P9-CFE-670

Milt & Marty

ALSO BY TOM LEOPOLD

Almost Like Being Here

Somebody Sing

Milt & Marty

The Longest Lasting & Least Successful
Comedy Writing Duo in Show Biz History

||||||||||||||||||||||||||||||||||||||||||||||||||||||

TOM LEOPOLD
& BOB SAND

||||||||||||||||||||||||||||||||||||||||||||||||||||||

MILT & MARTY. Copyright© 2008 by Tom Leopold and Bob Sand. All rights reserved. Published in the United States by Virgin Books. No part of this book may be used or reproduced in any manner whatsoever without written permission except in the case of brief quotations embodied in critical articles and reviews. For information, address Virgin Books, 65 Bleecker Street, New York, NY 10012.

Distributed by Macmillan

This is a work of fiction. All of the characters, companies, organizations, and events are either the products of the authors' imagination or used fictitiously and are not to be understood as real.

FIRST EDITION

Designed by Jason Snyder

Library of Congress Cataloging-in-Publication Data
Leopold, Tom.
    Milt & Marty : the longest lasting & least successful comedy writing duo in show biz history / Tom Leopold & Bob Sand.—1st ed.
        p. cm.
    ISBN-13: 978-1-905264-18-6
    ISBN-10: 1-905264-18-6
    1. Comedy—Authorship—Fiction. 2. Television comedy writers—Fiction. 3. Motion picture industry—Fiction. 4. Losers—Fiction. 5. Comedians—Fiction. 6. Hollywood (Los Angeles, Calif.)—Fiction. I. Sand, Bob. II. Title. III. Title: Milt and Marty.
    PS3562.E59M55 2008
    813'.54—dc22   2008001289

10 9 8 7 6 5 4 3 2 1

For Barbara, Olivia, Augusta,
and everybody's favorite dog, Henry
—Tom

For Barbara McCaslin-Sand, with love
—Bob

"Never give up. Never, never, never, never, ever give up!"

—Winston Churchill, explaining in his diary, in the winter of 1943, his philosophy regarding how long he planned to continue stalking screen star Greer Garson

NEVER MADE
THE BLACKLIST

IIIIIIIIIIIIIIIIIIIIIIIII

O f the hundreds of thousands of boys who graduated from American high schools in 1967, only two of them, Tom Leopold and Bob Sand, opted to pass up various drunken grad night celebrations—the co-ed pool parties, the stag movie circle-jerk competitions in somebody's brother-in-law's basement, and the romantic, overpriced Manhattan dinners with the virginal girlfriends—in favor of staying at Tom's house and watching *The Joe Franklin Show* broadcast live from a porn- and crime-riddled corner of Times Square on WOR-TV, Channel 9. Whereas most other male graduates cared deeply about stockpiling as many graduation night memories as possible, Leopold and Sand cared only about show biz, the embodiment of which was Joe Franklin, a man who had transformed himself from Joseph Fortgang of the Bronx into the poor man's Johnny Carson or even poorer man's Merv Griffin.

Leopold, a seventeen-year-old, 107-pound anorexic boy—the first of his generation, according to the records of the now defunct Michigan-based Jewish-American Eating Disorders Research Institute—made a point of sitting in the autumn-toned den of his family's luxurious home on Jersey City's ritzy Bentley Avenue, every night, and inhaling the entirely cornball, occasionally smarmy, but always fascinating Joe Franklin experience just inches from the brand-new state-of-the-art Zenith color TV for which his father, a frustrated entertainer turned successful dress manufacturer who could never forgive himself for not having become an even more successful hat manufacturer—"the milliners, Tommy, they're the ones with the magic"—had paid cold cash. Meanwhile, Tom's best friend, Bob Sand, also seventeen, a 207-pound "big-boned" boy with an unusually large cranium, was alone over on the wrong side of the tracks, with his size 9⅝ head cocked at an odd angle atop his fleshy pink shoulders in his Jersey City slum apartment, after having just gotten off the phone with his hedonist, physical culturist bodybuilder of a father, Lou Sand, a Bronx-born Jew who worked six nights a week, three hundred nights a year, as a galavanting professional wrestler known as Chief Crazy Eagle of the Great Apache Nation.

Bob's apartment was the same one in which he'd been living on the infamous morning, during his twelfth year of life, when his mother abandoned him and his father and headed to Alabama to begin her ultimately unsuccessful pursuit of iconic circus clown Emmett Kelly—to whom she referred, although she'd never met him, as "the love of my life!"—after which Bob would see her only once more.

After hanging up the phone with his father, Sand tried to put his genetic damage behind him long enough to rush outside, leap onto his ten-year-old Huffy Convertible bicycle, and pedal like a maniac through the mean streets of Jersey City in order not to miss the very same *Joe Franklin* segment Tom was preparing to watch over on the advantaged side of town. Had Bob not made the effort to get to Tom's house on time, he would have had to watch the show by himself on a nine-inch black-and-white set that his father had picked up as part of a Fort Hesterly, Florida, Studebaker dealer's free-with-oil-change promotion, and which would eventually be recalled for its tendency to explode up to an hour after it had been turned off. And, what's worse, he also would have broken the pact he and Tom had made, back in freshman year, to watch every *Franklin* show together, regardless of whatever else happened to be going on in their lives.

The boys were different in ways even more profound than the screen sizes of their TVs. For example, Tom's mother—a beautiful woman who'd never gotten over the abuse she'd taken from her peers as a chubby preteen and insisted, whenever she wore a new bathing suit out to the family pool, that Tom and his father "drive around the block until I'm neck-deep in the shallow end!"—never ran away in search of the love of a famous sad clown, choosing instead to stay at home with her husband and son, with whom she spent only high-quality hours. It broke her heart to learn that her beloved boy may have inherited her weight obsession.

Tom had become clinically sad during his sixth year of grade school when he found it impossible to achieve the level of slenderness he so admired in some of his school's nuevo anorexics. The weight-obsessed teenaged subculture of which Tom so yearned to be a part would meet each day behind the gym at Tom's private Jersey City academy to surreptitiously try on each other's chinos and vie for zipping rights, which were awarded to whomever least needed to hold his stomach in. The winner would then get bus fare to the local ice cream parlor for a victory gorge 'n' puke. When Tom's dad heard that Tom had been recruited as a lower-grade chino holder, he made a point of taking more time to "hang out with, and get closer to" his son. The two got so close, as a matter of fact, that his dad demanded they celebrate Tom's sixteenth birthday by having simultaneous nose jobs in adjoining ORs, and then recuperate together in the same hospital room, where Tom's mother found them lighting up celebratory cigars in horrifying proximity to their actively hissing oxygen tanks.

Sadly for Bob, the only person other than Tom with whom he'd ever had the chance to hang out, during his all-important teen years, wasn't a person at all but a dog. In an attempt to respond to the residual loneliness Bob was still feeling two years after his mother ran away, Lou had bought his then fourteen-year-old son a dog. Bob named the dog Brownie, and he loved it so much that it was as if the seemingly permanent darkness might soon begin to lift from his soul. Unfortunately, Lou showed up at the apartment on the day after Brownie had become a member of the family to find a steaming little puppy pile of b.m. on the bathroom throw rug. When Bob got home from school that day there was no more Brownie and not even one trace that a Brownie had ever been there. Every artifact from the dog's brief appearance in Bob's life—the bowl, the dog food, the puppy toys, the pee pads, the Arf-Arf Multi-Flavored Crunchy Treats—had been removed and Lou denied that any Brownie had ever existed.

"You must be imagining things, kid," he told his son, at which moment Bob began his Olympics-qualifying triple gainer inward.

He started writing fiction, for one thing, his first effort being a short story called "Now You See It, Now You Don't" about "a traveling magician who makes certain people, and other beloved living things, disappear." Instead of mailing the story to *The New Yorker*, which was already his favorite magazine, Bob sent it to the Hotel Chase in St. Louis, where his father was about to begin a series of matches against various men who, over the course of Lou's next twelve weeks of employment as a make-believe Indian chief, would be making believe they were cowboys, Arab sheikhs, mysterious masked men from Parts Unknown, bleached blonde Hollywood beach bums, and other Indian chiefs from competing tribes. Bob hoped, as he explained to his father in an attached note, that Lou would, after reading the story, "seek the psychiatric help you so desperately need" so that the two of them might, at some point in the future, reunite. Until then, Bob wrote, he would be "heading out into the world on my own, just like you did when your father broke your heart." By not mentioning to his father that the actual world he was heading out into was the guest suite that had been constructed from nine hundred square feet of "extra, unused space" in Tom's semifinished basement, Bob was practicing the art of denial—pretending that Lou didn't really know him well enough to be able to figure out in an instant where he'd headed out to. But when the phone rang, on his second night at Tom's place, Bob ran to answer it himself, explaining to Mrs. Leopold, who'd been marveling at the staggering width and breadth—"can you imagine how much information he's able to keep stored in that thing?"—of Bob's skull, that "I recognize my father's ring."

"Hello?" he said into the phone.

"If I'd known you wanted a dog that bad, kid," said his father on the other end of the line, "I woulda bought you one."

"You did buy me one."

"Don't do that."

"Don't do what?"

"Talk crazy like that when I'm half a country away."

"You're gonna play the game forever, aren't you?"

"What game?"

"The 'There Was No Brownie' game."

"But there was no Brownie."

After he and Lou hung up on each other, Bob couldn't believe that he hadn't told him he had in his possession a Polaroid photograph—which had been taken through a window without his knowledge by their eighty-eight-year-old neighbor Mary Feeney—that captured him and Brownie leaving their building together for what would turn out to be the only walk the two of them would ever share.

Despite their difference in head size, Tom and Bob shared an important similarity in addition to their devotion to Joe Franklin: both had always been funny. Not that anyone—not even their parents—had ever known it. Shy beyond words, the boys had retreated into a world where their common passion—professional comedy and the people who made their living doing it—was worshipped and dreamed about and coveted in secret, like some buried treasure that each had read about but neither believed he would ever actually hold in his hands. By the age of fifteen Bob had already transformed himself into a character his second best friend at the time, Joey Verdiramo, called the Wandering Jew Who Wanted in Show Biz in the Worst Fucking Way. With the clothes he'd bought at the Jersey City Hadassah Ladies Auxiliary Thrift Store on Journal Square, he built a writer's outfit—brown tweed jacket, gray flannel pants, black turtleneck sweater, and brown half-boots—which he wore on his regular walking tours of Manhattan, which town, he felt in his heart, he and his talent would one day conquer. Tom likewise had, by the same age, already begun to study comedians in an attempt to figure out how their jokes and funny stories had been constructed, why some of the lines worked and some of them didn't, and how much impact delivery, timing, and the intangible known as presence, or complete lack of same, helped or hindered the comedian who lived or died by them. Tom was doing his own preparation, too, practicing his delivery on the very first joke he'd ever written—which, to his amazement and joy, had made his maid fall down in the den with laughter. "My Uncle Seymour never wore socks his whole life," he said, clutching his mother's Princess Phone Microphone, "'cause he said he wanted his feet to breathe. People made fun of him, but it turned out that he knew what he was talking about. Uncle Sy died in 1953 but his feet lived till the spring of 1961."

Had Bob not been standing at a urinal in the Snyder High boys' room, back in 1964, when he overheard Tom reciting from Redd Foxx's comedy record *You Gotta Wash Your Ass!* behind his closed stall, the two boys, who were in different freshman homerooms, might never have met. And had Tom and Bob's obsessive New York show biz night trawling expeditions not later led them to a Manhattan institution called the Gagwriters' Comedy Workshop, they might never have been inspired to perform, to medium but still thrill-giving laughs, the Ralph Kramden–Ed Norton "Chef of the Future" sketch from *The Honeymooners*. And if they hadn't done that, neither would then have had the necessary courage to perform the same sketch during their high school's Senior Talent Night, where the response was better than it had been at the workshop (only two boys from special ed yelled "Eat me! You suck!" at them). Because of their appearance at the Snyder High talent show, Tom and Bob were able to enjoy, during the final three days of their senior year, the only popularity they'd ever known in high school.

That everyone in their school suddenly realized they were funny meant less to both than the fact that each considered the other to be funny, which was meaningless to them in light of the fact that the one person in their respective worlds whose similar acknowledgment would have made all the difference in that world—their fathers—never offered it. But, then again, had Tom and his parents not been watching an appearance by a Hungarian father-son acrobatic team on *The Ed Sullivan Show* when Tom was nine—and if Tom hadn't laughed at how silly the nine-year-old boy on TV looked in his girly costume—Tom's father would not have uttered the eight words that devastated and motivated him (and filled him with the same burning determination never finishing a meal once did) to get into show business at any cost. Those eight words? "Laugh, kid, but he's there and you're *here!*"

Accompanied by a bar mitzvah prereception snack table's worth of potato chips, mixed nuts, cookies, pretzels, caramels, licorice, Nik-

L-Nips, sodas, candy bars, and freezing-cold bottles of Yoo-hoo choco-
late drink for Bob and a can of Fresca with a side of cottage cheese
(small curd) for Tom, the two readied themselves for their one hundred and fourth consecutive viewing of *The Joe Franklin Show*.

"Hul-lo, my friends, and welcome to Joe Franklin's Memory Lane,"
said the wide-tied, maroon polyester–blazered, asymmetrical haircuted
Mr. Joe Franklin himself. "Tonight on our show we are honored to be
graced with a dazzling array of excellent guests, so please join me in wel-
coming, first, an old friend of ours, the mysterious mentalist known as
El Thinko, who made himself famous in the Catskill Mountains, back in
1948, for hailing cabs with his mind." Joe talked about how he couldn't
get a taxi in the rain, which segued (in typically odd Franklin fashion)
to how there's never a cop around when you need one . . . a tact that led
Joe absolutely nowhere so he turned back to his guest for a life line. "Do
you still do that, El Thinko? Still hail taxis with thoughts alone?"

"I did it t'night, Joe," said El Thinko, in his thick Brooklyn accent.
"How d'ya think I got t' the studio?"

Ignoring the chuckles coming from the cameraman and a hand-
ful of other disembodied backstage voices, Joe Franklin continued.

"Also with us this evening, for the very first time, are the fabulous
Stank and Drek—Mona Stank and Monty Drek, by name—a husband
and wife team of death-defying precision daredevil ice skaters who, I
am told, are famous for cutting perfect veal cutlets with their blades."

"Great to be here, Joe!" said Stank and Drek, as if they were one.

"And we also have with us our old friend Mr. Larry Geitz, a President Eisenhower impersonator who insists on keeping his act going
today, which is more than six years after Ike left office, which compels
me to ask a question of Mr. Geitz. Why?"

"'Why,' Joe?"

"I mean why continue with a thing that some people—many people—might consider to be no longer so-cial-ly re-le-vant, as the beatniks might call it?"

"Ike was a great general and a great president and a great man, Joe," said Larry Geitz. "And I intend to impersonate him till the day I die."

"And how old are you now?"

"Forty-six."

"Forty-six," repeated Joe Franklin, who then stared into the camera and said, "So be on the lookout, ladies and gentlemen, over the course of the next fifty years or so, God be willing, for Mr. Larry Geitz, America's most loyal President Eisenhower impersonator extraordinaire."

Back in Jersey City, Tom and Bob were laughing so hard at the beauty and perfection of Franklin's oddball lineup—not to mention the man's own hyperearnest delivery—that they missed the beginning of Joe's introduction of Milt and Marty.

"And finally, my friends, last but not least we have with us, also for the first time, a comedy writing team by the name of Mr. Marty Sloyx-nee and his partner—"

"It's Sloyxne!" shouted Marty through the spittle-shooting jester's yap stuck in the large round face set atop the massive, ovoid body beneath the long, wildly unkempt red hair.

"I beg your pardon?" said Joe Franklin.

"You said 'Sloyx-nee,' Joe. You made the mistake of pronouncing the 'x' but it's 'Sloyxne,' as in 'Sloyne,' with a silent 'x.'"

"Oh," said Joe Franklin. "So the 'x' is silent?"

"As silent as it comes," said Marty. "I am known in our wonderful business as Marty 'The X Is Silent!' Sloyxne."

"So the 'x' is definitely silent, then."

"Yes it is."

"So why keep it in the name? Good question, right?" Joe was excited with himself.

Milt and Marty remained silent but the crew chuckled at that one, and Tom and Bob roared.

"And here tonight with Mr. Marty Sloyxne with the silent 'x' is his writing partner, Mr. Milt Wagonman, who I don't think has any silent letters, if I'm not mistaken, correct me if I'm wrong."

"No, Joe, you're absolutely right," said a skinny, delicate, wispy-haired, doe-eyed, hypernervous, ghostly pale, profusely perspiring, assless Milt Wagonman. "Nothing in my name is pronounced."

"You mean nothing in it is *silent*," corrected Joe Franklin.

"Yes," said Milt.

"And Misters Wagonman and Sloyxne with the silent 'x,'" said Joe, moving right along, "whose career as a team started on radio writing *Frenchy the Ghost* starring the now totally dead Charles Boyer, have the distinction of having been rejected, as my spies tell me, by the Communist Party, which a number of years ago they tried to join but were told by some unnamed comrade, maybe Larry Parks himself, that they hadn't achieved—and I'm quoting here—'a sufficiently impressive set of show business credentials to be voted in.' Would you care to expound on that for our fans, gentlemen?"

"Most assuredly," said an affable Milt.

"We only wanted to be communists so we could get blacklisted, Joe!" said an unaffable Marty. "It's important for your viewership to appreciate that. I killed a Jap by my own methods. I'll put my patriotism up against anybody!"

True, in 1954 Wagonman and Sloyxne were so low on the show biz totem pole that they couldn't even get themselves blacklisted during the Hollywood witch hunt of that era, a slight that drove the team to try to join the Communist Party but only to be able to say, if anyone asked, that *that* was why they were unemployed. Their dream was to be grilled by Senator Joseph McCarthy during the HUAC hearings on national television—"a hopefully career-ruining event," as they put it, which they then expected to parlay into much more work under assumed names than they had ever been able to get under their own.

"We're having good conversation, gentlemen . . . and a history lesson," said Joe Franklin. "I am also told, in that case, that you and Mr. Wagonman have the distinction of being considered to be the longest-lasting, least successful comedy writing duo in the history of our business. To last that long without big-time success. That's got to be a feather in your cap gentlemen, no? Yes? What?"

"Most assuredly," said a still affable Milt.

"We've had more success than two people who slice veal with their skates!" said Marty, even less affable than before. "How 'bout talking about the good things me and my partner do, Joe, like how we sponsor the Wagonman and Sloyxne Young Comedy Writers Competition every year?"

"Okay," said Joe Franklin. "I am anxious for you to expound on that, you've got to help the youth, they're the hope. Aren't the youth the hope El Thinko?" But El Thinko was too busy patting his trousers to make sure he still had his wallet to hear Joe's question.

"We love to expound, Joe," said Marty, who then looked into the camera and said, as if talking to his own troubled child, "Me and Milt know you're out there, talented young unproduced comedy writer! We know you're out there, and we know you're funny, and we know that, regardless of your talent, nobody is givin' you the time of day. Which is why we want you to send us your material! Send all your unperformed, unproduced jokes, sketches, situation comedy and movie scripts, along with any loose change and funny prose, to Wagonman and Sloyxne, in care of the Cyclops Tavern, 4418 Hollywood Boulevard, Hollywood,

California. Please be advised that, because of mailing costs, we will not, at this time, be able to return the material."

"Do you offer a prize to the winner?" asked Joe Franklin.

"Most assuredly!" said a suddenly affable Marty. "Everyone who enters the competition will receive an autographed copy of *Who Spiked the Punch Line?*, an encyclopedia of killer jokes even a schmuck could get a laugh with. *Plus* an eight-by-ten photo of me and Milt eating sand dabs at our regular table at the famous Brown Derby restaurant with the chief judge of our competition, Mr. Arthur Glenn."

"Who's Arthur Glenn?" asked Joe Franklin.

"He's the towel guy at the Hollywood Y," said Milt.

"He used to be the prop guy for Spike Jones, really knows comedy," said Marty.

Back in Jersey City, Bob asked Tom, who was scribbling furiously on the front page of that day's *Journal-American*, "Did you get all that?"

"Got it!" said Tom. "Hollywood, here we come!"

It's amazing to consider that, even at the midway point of their careers, Milton Abraham Lincoln Wagonman and Marty (The X Is Silent!) Sloyxne were still being hounded by the "Longest Lasting and Least Successful Comedy Writing Duo in Show Biz History" rap. Not that the boys weren't a justifiable 50 percent proud of the moniker. Or, as the torturously upbeat Milt said, "Remember, Martin, better to be 50 percent proud in a business you love than 510 percent proud in a real line of work!" To which Marty replied, "First of all, you stupid douche, nobody can be 510 percent proud of anything. A person can only be 110 percent proud of anything, 110 percent is the top, the limit, the ceiling God put on numbers to signify the whole. It's the simple law of physical mathematics, for Christsweetsakes!"

Once the masterful Joe Franklin got Marty calmed down, and his devoted makeup people did what they could to powder away the white foam of rage still clinging to Marty's upper lip, the interview sailed right along. Even if you take into consideration Marty's eleven-minute diatribe wherein he compared the Salvadorans to "syphilitic monkey beings who, in all likelihood, will never leave a significant mark on the American comedy business!"—a rant stemming from Marty having spent much of the day trying to have his Salvadoran hair colorist deported. In the poor woman's excitement over Marty's big break "on the televisions!" the beautician mistakenly hennaed his long, wild hair with Sunrise in Cairo Red instead of Marty's usual Cleveland Industrial Park Red.

Milt, as was his habit, had arrived at Franklin's studio his customary four hours early with Gwen, his sainted wife, by his side. The decade-out-of-date but eternally dapper Wagonman's only misstep was insisting on wearing his lucky pants on the program. Milt had been married in the trousers, had been kicked extremely hard in the seat of them by the great Bing Crosby himself who'd felt that Milt's ass resembled the ass of his laziest son, and had even worn them on the day he walked his daughter, Randi, to her first day at nursery school, years before the child grew up, joined the lesbians, and stole the transmission out of his Buick. Because Milt's pants held such an honored place in his heart, he wouldn't even allow Gwen to wash them, fearing that she might "rinse all the lucky out."

If, as is often said, show business is all timing, what then were the odds that ol' Lady Luck would choose the night of the *Franklin* show to split the frayed crotch seams on Milt's lucky pants to the point of fully exposing the large, white lump of his failed hernia truss to Joe's entire tri-state viewership whenever Milt crossed or uncrossed his legs? Milt's ill-timed truss/lump exposure, along with the mean-spirited bile of Marty's Salvadoran hate rant, left the team of Wagonman and Sloyxne a scant forty-eight seconds of air time to explain their love of mirth.

"My thanks to Mr. Marty 'The X Is Silent!' Sloyxne and his partner, Mr. Milt Wagonman," said a visibly—and uncharacteristically—irritated Joe Franklin, "who have now had more uninterrupted air time—and please correct me if I'm wrong, someone in the booth—than anyone else in the history of this program. But it is now time to find out some of the doings and not-doings of our other guests, so—"

"Ladies and gentlemen," Marty continued, waving Franklin off. "If a writer is fortunate enough to hear his jokes come to life, well, it's a fabulous thing for a person. And I know I speak for my partner when I say this, so there'll be no reason for him to open his yap . . ."

The *Franklin* audience of nine believed, mistakenly, that Marty was only joking, but Gwen, Milt's long-suffering wife, knew the truth and shot her husband a supportive thumbs-up from the wings, which Milt, who was terribly nearsighted, mistook as a call for him to hike up his pants, which succeeded only in exposing more of his truss.

As though summoning wisdom from a comedy muse hovering just above the stage of the old, damp Joe Franklin Theater, Marty gazed up at the ceiling for dramatic emphasis. "If I may take one more moment of your time, Mr. and Mrs. John Q. American Viewing Public, I'd like to add that all we witsmiths can do is point you people, like dumb animals, to something wonderfully funny. But if you choose not to laugh at the fruits of our comedy labors, then, how in God's name is that our fault?" At this point Marty, who'd caught a whiff of the gas he'd involuntarily set loose upon the world, reached in his pocket, removed and opened a pack of matches, struck a courtesy flame, and held it to the back of his slacks in an effort to smite the outrage at its source. At the same time he lost his train of thought, which caused him to ask Franklin, "By the way, Joe, did we mention what a thrill it is to be here?"

Milt & Marty

While the boom operator wondered how long it would take for Marty's pants to burst into flames, Franklin seized the opportunity to move his chair a little farther away from Marty and ask Milt a question, which was, "Why, Mr. Wagonman—and I don't often ask questions like this one—have you lasted so long as this man's partner?"

Always eager to go toe-to-toe with anyone, Marty blew out the match and replied, "Mr. Wagonman has been able to last with me, Joe, because he and I have been given a wonderful gift by God that does not work as well, for each of us, as individuals but comes to its own mysteriously magical, chemical life as a team. Although my gift is more the funny, whereas Milton's more of a structure guy." Milt nodded, happy to be included in any way at all. "The ability to think up the kind of world-class comedy you've witnessed, even in this brief venue, ladies and gentlemen," said Marty, "well, an audience could never find the words to thank us for it because you have not been given a gift of God like us."

Milt chimed in, "But if you had been given the gift and were able to express that gratitude? I'm sure Marty would join me in replying that it has been an honor to entertain you."

Marty was forced to rise above Milt's interruption, when, for the first time that evening, he allowed himself the hope that his appearance on *Franklin* might actually get him laid. The reason for his newfound hope was that there was an extremely plain-faced woman among the show's crew who had been giving him the eye. And if there was anything on God's green earth that made Martin Sloyxne harder than Chinese mathematics, it was the sight of an extremely plain-faced woman.

Wondering if the plain-faced woman was quite plain enough forced him to yield the stage to El Thinko, who went on to captivate the bewildered audience with a nine-minute story about a Hindu mystic who had so deeply hypnotized a crowd of Untouchables bathing in the Ganges that a mass hallucination was induced wherein they all, men and women alike, began to believe they were Burt Lancaster appearing in the film *Trapeze*.

"Imagine it deeply, gentle people," El Thinko went on to say in a voice so mellifluous that Milt started to feel like Burt Lancaster too. "Imagine it very deeply," El Thinko whispered-spoke-sung. "Twelve hundred of the poorest of the poor gripping an imaginary trapeze bar as oxen and sacred fly-covered cows made up the audience for their fantasy circus."

Marty elbowed Milt sharply in the ribs to break the whammy El Thinko had put on his partner, but it was to no avail. "Damn it, Mr. Ringling North!" Milt suddenly yelled in what had to be the worst Burt Lancaster impression ever attempted. "I'm going to give you that triple somersault, Mr. Ringling North! I'm going to give it to you because . . . that's *circus*!"

As a dead-eyed Milt rose zombielike from his chair, his lucky pants fell completely away, leaving him, from the waist down, clad only in his truss, which in the hot television lights resembled the briefs Lancaster had actually worn in the film. Milt then jumped in the air, took hold of a light rigging bar just above his head, and began to swing, gaining speed, quickly, back and forth, over the audience.

Even an old pro like Joe Franklin was hard-pressed to know what the hell to do at this point. As Milt's swinging gained in altitude, some in the audience began to hope that the old comedy writer would actually accomplish the triple somersault he promised an invisible John Ringling North, while others just sat there stunned, hoping Milt's truss wouldn't drop on their heads.

"Milton, what in shit's name are you doing? You're going to kill yourself," Marty barked at him as Gwen Wagonman clutched her heart. Security was called and Joe Franklin shouted for El Thinko to order an ambulance with his mind before anyone got seriously hurt.

Finally, Larry Geitz, the presidential impressionist, sighed and said in a voice that sounded nothing like Ike, "I wonder if anyone is still watching this—whatever it is."

"My fans are nothing but loyal," said Franklin, and he was right, for at least two people—Tom Leopold and Bob Sand—were, at that very moment, glued to Tom's TV screen in the faux avocado–paneled den of the big house in Jersey City, desperate for more, ribs aching, inspired (although slightly grossed out by the truss) by Milt and Marty's mad but oddly noble commitment to the comedy moment. They were quietly sure, for the first time ever, that it was time to make their big move.

MILTON BERLE'S GRANDSON

IIIIIIIIIIIIIIIIIIIIIIIIIII

S ince Milt and Marty never responded to the sketch Tom and Bob stuck in the mail to them two hours after that *Franklin* show aired (a ten-page piece about Hugh Hefner losing control of his car and driving through a suburban living room where a Tupperware party is in progress), they decided, on their own, that the material's quality was of such a high order they didn't need college to fall back on and headed straight for Hollywood. Once settled in a suitable hovel they signed up for a class—"Surviving in the TV Sitcom Writing Jungle: How to Do It, How Not to Do It, and What to Do Next if Mr. Smalnitz Tells You You're the Real Thing!"—that was being offered at the UCLA night-class extension by a veteran semisuccessful sitcom producer named Norman Smalnitz.

Not long after writing an essay called "Woody Allen Never Needed to Take a Class" Leopold and Sand would be offered a one-day trial shot by Smalnitz to come in and help him punch up his latest pilot script. Tom and Bob were told by the "young Turk fresh out of the mail room" William Morris subagent they went to for advice that if Smalnitz's pilot gets picked up as a series—which, he said, "has about as much chance of happening as Leonard Nimoy growing a twat"—Smalnitz might hire them as staff writers on it, and that he, the subagent, might sign them as clients, which, he said, "has about as much chance of happening as John Wayne keeping his own set of kosher dishes."

On the morning of their very first day in show business—Monday, February 9, 1968—Tom Leopold and Bob Sand showed up at Room 104 of the Mae West Building at Paramount Studios in Hollywood to help punch up a CBS pilot script called *Give Your Uncle Back His Legs*, which was scheduled to be filmed, on the following Monday night, before a live audience of inmates from Chino state prison. The script had been written by writer-producer Smalnitz, who had apparently "seen that unseeable something" in the boys. The unseeable something the producer had seen was their eagerness to work for what he called "very little money," while helping him add jokes to his script during the week before one of his certain-not-to-make-the-fall-network-schedule pilot productions started. Tom and Bob soon learned that "very little money" was actually a euphemism for "zero money," but at least they'd gotten their feet in the door and, regardless of the fact that they were required to park, every morning, nine blocks from the nearest entrance to the lot in a seedy Paramount-owned structure, they were touching their dream.

Give Your Uncle Back His Legs was a period piece about Gus, a double-amputee veteran of World War II—the "uncle" of the title, who lived in 1946 Long Island with his widowed sister-in-law and her ten-year-old son, Andrew, the amputee's nephew, his dead brother's kid, who hated the uncle because the uncle's entire focus, his reason for being, was to schtup the kid's mother—which the kid was never going to let happen, making him heroic, in a way. He protected his mother—the most naive, innocent woman ever to come to semilife in the pages of a sitcom script—by hiding his uncle's prosthetic legs at night so that his uncle couldn't go into his mother's bedroom and "do nasty things on her." As lame as the idea sounded to them, Tom and Bob took it seriously because it was part of the Business, and because the idea of having to work in "the civilian world," as they called it, gave each of them such loose stool that they would have embraced an even more depressing show biz opportunity. The possibility that they might be thrown in, on their first day of work, with a twelve-pack of vicious, aging comedy-writing jackals—Smalnitz's Big Nutz, they called themselves—didn't even occur to them. Which is too bad, because the minute the two baby writers walked in the room the veteran jokesmiths went for the jugular.

"Did someone here order a pair of fags?" shouted Marvin Tiknik, barely looking up from his Hollywood Park tout sheet.

"I ordered fags," said his partner, Lenny Precht. "But I said 'handsome'!"

The mean-spirited veterans were trying, as they'd tried many times before with other rookie writers, to discourage the young bright-eyed, hope-engorged Tom and Bob from trying to remain in show business for more than the nine minutes they'd already put in. They wanted, in the grand tradition of all hacks, for Tom and Bob to feel that they were worthless, out-of-place pieces of dog shit with nothing interesting about them besides the depth of their naïveté—and it was working.

Then, just as Tom and Bob's immune systems began to shut down, there emerged from out of the ooze one lone, gentle voice belonging to a skinny gentleman who looked to be in his mid-fifties, who said to his peers, "Hey, fellas, come on, now, wouldja? Wouldja leave the baby writers the heck alone, now, please, doggoneit? Cuz if you don't, I'll tell Sloyxne when I see him what you done, and the results to you pleasing I swear to God they will not be. Does the word 'blood' ring the bell of truth?"

To the boys' amazement, the old writers, in spite of the fact that the fifty-something gentleman had just kneed the English language in the balls, respected what he had said enough to return their figurative knives to their respective life-despairing sheaths and withdrew. As soon as the other writers were out of earshot, their champion told the brand-new team that "the guys finally stopped it already with the sadism when they heard the name 'Sloyxne' because Marty scares the ever lovin' mud outa all o' them."

All Tom and Bob could do was stare, for it was at that moment each realized that the person who'd saved them from certain show business death was none other than Milt Wagonman, who happened to have been 50 percent responsible for reenforcing their show business dreams back on the *Joe Franklin Show*.

Two of the many negative things for which Marty Sloyxne, Milt's partner, was known was never being on time on the first day of any job—it was a source of pride with him—and for being a savage homicidal maniac to anyone he suspected of taking advantage of—or insulting, or disrespecting, or being condescending toward, or looking down upon, or ignoring, or taking the dessert of, or diminishing the value of—the weak. If he saw anyone doing that he could be dangerous. And his peers knew it. Word had it that he'd once head-butted legendary chanteuse Edith Piaf in the face backstage at one of her Carnegie Hall concerts in the fifties because she wouldn't autograph the "I Love Sparrows!" embossed boys' underpants being worn by Marty's then ten-year-old, emotionally disturbed son, Raymond. From that night on, Marty hated the French with a passion—which meant that they suddenly had something in common with the Italians, the Irish, the Mexicans, the British, the Germans, the North and South Africans, the Australians, the Hawaiians, the Scottish, the Fiji Islanders, the Belgians, the Swiss, the Swedish and Norwegian and Danish and the Dutch as well as his fellow Americans and his fellow Jews, in addition to the girl next door and bushy-haired scientists and all dogs and cats and rabbis and priests and doctors and cops and firemen (Irish and Italian) and insurance agents and "made to order" shoe salesmen and hunters and fly fishermen and lawyers and the young and the elderly and his fellow writers regardless of their race, creed, gender, national origin, or religious affiliation . . . especially his fellow writers. Marty despised his fellow writers more than any other group on earth. And the other boys in the room that morning, the ones who'd wanted Leopold and Sand dead, if for no other reason than the fact that their parents had met forty years after theirs did, knew it and so dreaded Sloyxne's wrath.

Had Milt Wagonman not spoken up for Tom and Bob when he did that day, Tom certainly would've left the building and the lot and run along Melrose to the Greyhound station on Vine Street and bought a one-way ticket to Jersey; Bob would've stayed in town and eaten an entire wedding cake for lunch. And speaking of lunch, after Milt invited Tom and Bob to join him and Marty for "a little repast'ilizing" at the Friars Club, each man was too excited to hear anything else. They didn't hear him, for example, when he mused about how neither of them had spoken a single word "during your entire show biz debut morning. Not even after Tiknik and Precht and them other jerks had backed offa you, because you were too—whatchamacallit—intimidated to speak." And Tom and Bob didn't hear Milt when he chuckled about how Norman Smalnitz was "so ticked off" by their silence that he asked them, "Who were your fuckin' parents, boys—Helen Keller and the fuckin' Mummy?" Nor did Tom and Bob hear him when he told them that his partner, Marty, "has never met even one catatonic, let alone two," or when he said, "I think that when he hears about how terrified the two o' you were, it will most assuredly amuse the heck out of him with warmth, I really do."

No, all Tom and Bob heard, when Milt spoke the words "Friars Club," was the sound of their own hearts bouncing on the walls of their respective chest cavities like cold tenants begging for heat, for that was how big their hope to one day pass through the sacred portals of the Friars had always been.

"Hop in my new car, fellas," said Milt, pointing toward the Paramount lot at a used fire-engine-red '66 Falcon with no backseat, of which he was so proud because it was the first car he'd ever owned. "How d'ya like the paint job on her, boys?" he wanted to know. "Ain't she Rita Hayworth?"

"Beg your pardon, Mr. Wagonman?" said Tom.

"Did you say, 'Ain't she Rita Hayworth?'" asked Bob.

"It's what I do when I love," said Milt. "I turn gorgeous women that Frank Sinatra slept with into adjectives describing the love objects of which I am in love with. It means 'ain't she beautiful?'"

"She sure is," said Tom and Bob in unison.

"And for gosh almighty sakes, boys," said Milt. "Call me Milt already, before I hit you . . . Just kidding! About the hitting not the calling."

Before Milt turned his red Falcon over to a young, sexually confused aspiring actor who worked as a valet parking lot attendant at the Friars Club, he said, "Every doggoned ding and dent on the surface of this vehicle is something which I have committed to memory, young man, so please be as careful with it as you would your late grandmother's corpse."

The first thing the baby writers did on their way into the Beverly Hills Friars Club lobby was gasp as Phil Silvers, who was on his way out through the same door, bumped into them and said, "'A Star Is Jostled!' Coming soon to a theater near you!" And the first thing they did on their way into the Friars Club dining room was stop dead in their tracks at the sight of the 299-pound, half man–half Macy's Day Parade float known as Marty (The X Is Silent!) Sloyxne, who was already three-quarters of the way through a large seafood salad and sipping cocktail sauce through a straw as they approached his table.

"I got here early, pally," said Marty to Milt, "so I thought I'd have me a little appetizee." And then he looked at Tom and Bob, looked back at Milt, and asked, "What in my skid-marked shorts is this?"

"New baby writers on *Uncle*," said Milt. "They love our work."

"Oh yeah?" Marty asked, glancing the boys' way. "And which work might that be?"

Tom and Bob, who had no clue as to anything that Milt and Marty had ever done—unless they counted Milt revealing his truss on *The Joe Franklin Show*—were speechless for a few seconds before Milt bailed them out.

"*Grik, Grok, Gunk, Grunk, and Goo*," Milt said. "They adore the heck out of it."

This prompted Marty to stand up and sing, at the top of his lungs, the theme song to the 1958 NBC "Cave Era" series *Grik, Grok, Gunk, Grunk, and Goo*, on which he and Milt had worked as staff writers for all three episodes of its short life. With gusto and while still chewing, Marty sang.

"Who lives in this cold cave right here
In this land without a name?
Where fire was just invented
And nobody is tame?
Who gathers in the cold, cold night
And sniffs each other's hair?
And sits a caveman tush on freezing dirt
Because there ain't no chair?
Who picks off all their head lice

And sticks them on their tongues?

And tries to teach survival

To their helpless little youngs?

The answer it is simple

And the answer it is true

The answer my dear caveman is:

Grik, Grok, Gunk, Grunk, and Goo!"

"Shut the fuck up, Sloyxne!" yelled a voice from somewhere within the crowded dining room.

"You shut the fuck up, Burns!" yelled Marty in the direction of the voice. And then, turning to Tom and Bob, he whispered, "Ever since Gracie died, George has been one part national treasure and nine parts prick."

After lunch that afternoon—which, for Marty, was not limited to the aforementioned seafood salad but also included a standing rib roast—he stood up and left the table without saying a word and was still gone, forty minutes later, when Milt finally said, "Wonder where in the heck my partner is? Jeez, you don't think he got one of his cravings, do ya?"

"We don't even know what his cravings are, Mr . . . Milt," said Bob.

"Touché," said Milt.

Following what sounded to them like a dock fight in a tin can factory they found Marty in the kitchen, down on his hands and knees in the bread bin, being kicked over and over in the ass and ribs and lower back by the elderly pastry chef, for trying to satisfy one of his cravings by licking the sourdough rub off all the loaves of sourdough bread, which were acknowledged by those who knew their sourdoughs to be the best sourdough in the world, better, even—as long as they remained free of Marty or any other human being's saliva—than those at Musso and Frank's Famous Grill. The old pastry chef continued to kick at Marty's nuts until Milt and Tom and Bob had guided him about half the distance between the kitchen and the club's main entrance, at which point the chef ran out of wind, gasped, "I will see to it . . . that you . . . are never allowed . . . to set foot in . . . this club . . . again, Mr. Sloyxne!" and then fell to his knees with a partial stroke.

Unfortunately for Marty, the Friars maitre'd', a man who spoke with a British accent even though he'd been born and raised in Farmingdale, Long Island, and who had heard his beloved chef threaten Marty with banishment from the club before the left side of his face went slack, made the banishment official. "You are no longer welcome here, Mr. Sloyxne!" he said.

To which Marty replied, "Go fuck yourself, you triple-jointed queen!"

Back in the red Falcon Milt, who was furious with Marty, started telling him off, which shocked Tom and Bob. If the young partners didn't know any better, they might have thought that the older partners, with whom they were still as guardedly mesmerized as they'd been when they first saw them on television, might simply be lunatics. The thought chilled the younger partners, and they became even more chilled as Milt, who was normally the docile one in the Wagonman and Sloyxne zeitgeist, got more vociferous in his condemnation of Marty. The "simple" adjective was instantly dismissed when Tom and Bob learned that just two weeks earlier Milt caught Marty with his pants down—not to mention his underpants down—at Lucy's El Adobe Mexican restaurant on Melrose, kneeling in the big salt bin into which the waiters would dip the damp edges of their margarita glasses and depositing a primitive, feral, spermatozoal mess therein. Long story short, ladies and gentlemen, Mr. Sloyxne had orgasmed into the salt at the legendary Lucy's El Adobe.

"It was apparently his way," said a furious Milt to Tom and Bob, "of getting back at a certain waitress who, as far as he was concerned, had for several years been giving him lesser portions of the same meal—chicken enchiladas with salad, rice, and beans, the Number Four Combo, in other words—which he andx I had always ordered. 'She always gave you more,' he said. 'She always gave you more. Nah-nah-nah-nah-nah!'"

"But she always fuckin' did give you more!" shouted Marty. "Because you ain't fat and I am, and she despises the fuckin' fat!"

"You are a depraved, bread-licking, salt barrel–splorking miscreant!" shouted Milt at his partner, as the Falcon stopped at the red light at Wilshire and Santa Monica.

Where most insane men would have shouted back at Milt, Marty got a hang dog expression and said, "You're right, Milton. I know that I shouldn't have licked the rub off the bread or squirted my jungle juice into the margarita salt. I know that what I did in both cases was absolutely wrong, and I would like to make it up to you—and to our new baby writers, too, in the hope that they may enjoy at least as long and fulfilling a partnership as you and I have enjoyed—by suggesting to you that we call upon that which is most basic to our relationship, not to mention the strongest part of it—and I am speaking, of course, about our deep and profound respect and love for each other—by driving over to Milton Berle's house so that Tom and Bob can participate in a tradition as grand as show business itself. I am speaking, of course, of having them take a gander at Uncle Miltie's five-year-old grandson!"

Milt, fighting to hold on to his anger, shook his head and said, "No."

"Whaddya mean 'no'? It's a show biz tradition!"

"We have to get back to work," said Milt.

"It's lunch hour!"

"It's two-fifteen."

"We'll be back by three-thirty!"

Marty looked at the two baby writers and asked, "Whaddya say, boychiks? Y'wanna shit-can the rest of your first day in the biz and meet Uncle Miltie's five-year-old grandson? He's big for his age!"

"I'd rather meet Milton Berle," said Tom.

"Me too," said Bob.

At this point, Milt exploded in laughter even more incongruous to his persona than his bombastic outburst at Marty had been. This made Marty start "B-waaaaaaaaa!"-ing, which was the sound he made that came closest to the sound of normal, human laughter.

"What's so funny?" Tom wanted to know.

"Uncle Miltie's 'five-year-old grandson' is what I call his cock, fellas, bein' that it's the size of your average kindygarden student!"

Before either of them was able to form words, Tom and Bob found themselves standing outside Milton Berle's surprisingly modest-looking home.

"One thing, boys," said Marty, as he guided them toward Berle's front door. "Don't try and be funny or smart. If there's one thing Milton hates it's a pisher who thinks he's a maven."

And then, as if Berle's house was his own, Marty opened the door and entered the dwelling without first ringing or knocking, and Milt and Tom and Bob followed.

The minute Tom and Bob were inside, they knew something was amiss. The house seemed less palatial than any home either of them thought that someone like a Milton Berle would purchase. It was nice, but it didn't feel like it belonged to an iconic show business figure. For one thing, the walls were covered with Brooklyn Dodgers photographs and framed memorabilia, and there wasn't one photograph of Berle or anyone else in show business. Tom and Bob, who each counted three wheelchairs, also noticed an oxygen tank and multiple bottles of medication in the living room. They had recently seen Berle looking healthy and robust on TV, and they sensed that unless his wife was sick and they didn't know it—and they didn't think that there was any possible way they wouldn't have known it, what with their obsession with the details of the personal lives of famous funny people—they were in a home that didn't really belong to comedy icon Milton Berle.

Their theorizing was cut in two by the sound of Marty screaming at the top of his lungs, "Where the hell are ya, Uncle Miltie? I got two customers here for a shvontz sighting, Milton! Time to free the frightful beast from its cage!"

Followed closely by Tom and Bob and Milt, Marty began walking through the house, shouting Berle's name and opening doors like he owned the place. When Tom and Bob followed him onto the sun porch, they came face-to-face with none other than baseball legend Roy Campanella himself, sitting there in a wheelchair, sipping lemonade. As far as Tom and Bob were concerned, unless Roy Campanella was subletting from Milton Berle, they had entered the wrong house. Milt, whose face was flushed with embarrassment, started apologizing. "I'm sorry, Campy," he said. "I had no idea this was your lovely home."

Marty's feeling that he'd been backed into a corner intensified when Milt said, "He ain't Milton Berle, Marty . . . he's Roy Campanella, a Negro and the former star catcher for the Brooklyn Dodgers who, as you can plainly see, is now wheelchair-bound!" To which Marty responded by shouting at Milt, "Don't you get it, you naive fuck? This is what Berle looks like without the makeup! It's how he relaxes!"

Wagonman knew that the only way to get Sloyxne out of there—the only way, at this point, to let Marty save face, was for him to ask Campanella if it would be okay to pull his blanket down and let "the two new baby boy writers here" have a look at his penis—which meant that on their first day as Hollywood writers, Leopold and Sand were going to have to be Hollywood actors.

First, they were going to have to pretend that a black, paralyzed ex–baseball player was Milton Berle and that Campy's penis was Berle's penis, and then, regardless of what they really thought of the size of it, they were going to have to act amazed at its girth.

But Campy drew the line and refused to allow himself to be additionally humiliated.

"I'm afraid I can't let you do that, Marty," he said, as if he and Sloyxne knew each other. "I told you that the last time."

Marty, who was experiencing the rare phenomenon—for him—of speechlessness, glanced at Milt before storming off the sun porch and into the house like a petulant two-year-old.

Campanella looked at Milt and said, "I told him the last time he brought rookie writers over here that I wasn't gonna pretend to be Milton Berle, and I wasn't gonna let anyone look at my privates, man, and I told him he'd better not try that bush league stuff again!"

"I'm shocked, Campy," said Milt. "I had no idea that Marty had ever been here before. And I don't think he remembers it, either."

"Why's that? Is he a drunk?"

"No," said Milt. "He's complicated. A great many artists are. Mozart was complicated as well . . . Mozart and Marty."

"Man!" said Campy. "He's been here lots of times. He and I go way back together. I've known him since I began my playing days in the Negro League with the Baltimore Elite Giants. He used to hang around the clubhouse back then trying to get the players to sign an Impeach FDR petition. I got a real kick outa Marty's bullshit for the first twenty-five years, man, but I'm paralyzed now and it takes more than somebody mistaking me for a Jewish comedian, who I never thought was funny in the first place, to get a laugh outa me."

Roy Campanella, a true gentleman, remained gentlemanly, even after he'd wheeled himself from his sun porch to his living room to find Marty sitting in his whirlpool bath, watching his TV and eating his lunch.

When Milt saw Marty he was aghast. "What in the doggoned heck are you doing, Martin?" he said. "You've had two gigantic lunches already!"

"Who are you now?" Marty asked his partner. "Lunch judge?" And then, turning his gaze to Campanella, he said, "Campy, you got any party mix?"

Once again inside Milt's Red Falcon after "The Day We Didn't See Any Icon's Cock," as they would come to call it over the years, Tom and Bob felt many things, especially unbearable physical discomfort, being that they were the ones who had to crouch down in the vehicle's seatless rear area and would have to do so during what they thought would be the entire twenty-five-minute ride back to Paramount. As it turned out, though, the ride back to the studio would last another two hours. Marty insisted on taking "you wonderful little fuckin' wide-eyed, youth-drenched kids" on a tour of all of his and Milt's Hollywood–Burbank–LA–Beverly Hills haunts, including: Grauman's Chinese Theatre, and the Capitol Records building, and CBS, and NBC, and Farmers Market, and Cantors on Fairfax, and Nate 'n Al's on Beverly Drive, and the Beverly-Wilshire coffee shop. Each venue inspired an anecdote from Marty, and every anecdote was full of Marty's bitterness over some "big fuckin' macher" or "real Sammy fuckin' Glick" in the Business who had "treated me and my partner like a turd he tracked into his big house with the screening room!"

The only nonbitter tale Marty told the boys that day was inspired by the sight of the Beverly Hills Y, where, Marty said, he once saw a naked Lucille Ball towel-whipping a cowering Simone Signoret. "I seen her do it through a slit in my hidin' place inside one o' the ladies' locker room lockers, where I slept overnight in the hope of seein' Barbara Stanwyck—who I heard used t' like t' go swimmin' there every morning—with her clothes off. God, how I wanted to see what that woman looked like down south!"

While tooling through the rest of Beverly Hills that day, Milt drove the Falcon past a house on Bedford Drive where Martha Raye, the great 1940s comedienne, happened to be taking out her own trash. Responding to Marty's order, Milt backed up the Falcon and stopped parallel to Ms. Raye's house, at which point Marty rolled down his window, stuck his head out, and yelled, "Hey, Martha, how ya' doin', Sugar?"

Ms. Raye waved, smiled, and got back to her garbage, at which point Marty yelled, "Don't ya reco'nize me, Big Mouth? It's me! Marty Sloyxne!" At which point Ms. Raye, her face suddenly devoid of color, dropped her trash bag and ran screaming into her house.

"Can you believe that broad?" said Marty. "Talk about carrying a grudge!"

"Sure I can believe it," said Milt. "After all, you traumatized the poor woman during the war."

"When's she gonna f'give and fuckin' f'get, f' godsakes?"

"I'm afraid you're going to have to ask her that, Martin."

"Knob me, Cinderella!" Clearly Marty wanted the subject dropped.

"What did happen between you and Ms. Raye, anyway?" asked Bob.

"None o' your fuckin' business!" screamed Marty, his eyes red with rage.

"If you don't mind my asking," said Bob, hoping that Marty would be impressed enough with his timing to laugh, which the man was not.

"I do mind!" shouted Sloyxne. "Who the hell raised you anyway!"

"Nobody."

"Nobody? What d'you mean 'nobody'?"

"I mean my father was gone three hundred days a year, through-out my childhood, and my mother ran away when I was twelve."

"She ran away?" asked Marty, in a kind of hypersensitive doe voice.

"Yes."

"Where'd she go?"

"Wherever Emmett Kelly was."

"You mean the circus clown?"

"That's him."

Marty threw his head back, clutched his belly as though he'd been shot in the gut, bent over, and started dancing in place—in a way that made Tom and Bob think that, except for his height and weight, talent, age, skin color, and number of eyes in his head, he could very well have passed for Sammy Davis Jr.—and emitted, into the serene afternoon of Beverly Hills, a long and terrifying "B-waaaaaaahhhhhhhhhh!," thereby holding Milt and Tom and Bob, who had no choice but to sit out the three minutes it would take for the mad hyena laugh to run its course, captive.

"I'm pissin' myself over here!" said the depleted Marty, wiping tears from his eyes with one hand as his other reached back over the seat to clutch Bob's shoulder. "You are one funny prick, y' bastard. The choice of Emmett Kelly sold the bit. Absolutely *sold* it!"

"He wasn't being funny," said Tom in the middle of Sloyxne's seven-decibel, handkerchief-distorting nose blow.

"Huh?" snorted Marty, stopping short in mid-explosion. "He wasn't?"

"No. He was telling the truth."

"You mean she really abandoned him for Emmett Kelly?"

"Yes."

Turning to face Bob, Marty asked, with hot giant tears beginning to well in the dark and dissipated remainder store of disappointment that were his eyes, "Is what he says true, my boy? Your mama? Your mama-la? She left you for a clown? Tell me it isn't true! Speak before I drop dead from the sadness of it!" But before Bob could get to the first 't' in "It's true" Marty began to sob.

What Tom and Bob learned from Milt, after Marty had jumped out of the Falcon to begin what Milt described as "one of his grief walks; he takes one whenever his empathy for another living soul overwhelms him," was that he and Marty had met Martha Raye while they were writing USO shows overseas together during the war. Milt drove slowly so that Marty, who was walking alongside the car, would be able to hop back in when his Bob-grief had run its course.

"We wrote our first one together—'Red, White, and Jew'—the first week we knew each other," said Milt. "And it remains our favorite. We wrote it in response to a letter our company, which was comprised of mostly Jewish soldiers with show biz backgrounds, had received from the editors at this magazine, *The Jewish-American GI*, in response to the wave of anti-Semitism that, at that time, was sweeping through the military, not to mention the Gentile world, like wildfire, as opposed to today."

Tom and Bob laughed, but they could see, immediately, that Marty, who'd been listening to every word, didn't know why.

"Anyways," said Milt, as Marty got back in the car, "me and Marty wrote 'Red, White, and Jew' for six companies' worth of men—about twelve hundred GIs—and premiered it on February 2, 1944, on a stage set up on a pig farm in Caudebec-en-Caux, France. And it was great, beautiful, it went over just fabulous. A guy named Marvin Felt—who we used to tick off by saying, 'There he is, Marvin Felt, the only GI in the world whose name is a complete sentence!'—wrote the book and lyrics, and Rags Ragland played a patriotic moneylender who, although he was determined to beat the Axis powers, kept getting his nose caught—cuz we gave him a twenty-foot-long rubber nose, see, funnier than all get-out. He got it caught in Hirohito's paper door, which was our way of satirizing the fact that the Japs, they had them houses with paper walls and doors and what have you. There were great anti-hatred songs in it, too. 'Sheenies Ain't Meanies,' 'Wop the Heck Are You Lookin' At?,' 'Mick Me a Drink If You Would, Darling Dear,' 'Kraut's Just Somethin' I Slap on My Foot-long Dog,' 'Gook What I Brought You from Over There, Baby,' and 'Would Jew Like to Take a Walk,' among many others. And we didn't know it but Martha Raye, who was scheduled to do a show there on the following night, happened to be in the audience, with her hair up in her cap and sunglasses on her face, so's nobody would even know she was a woman, much less the great Martha Raye, and she loved it, she went nuts, and insisted on meeting 'the two idiots' who wrote the show. So we met her and became friends and she promised us that if we looked her up back in the States after the war she would give us work."

"Which she did not do!" shouted Marty.

"Why not?" asked Tom.

"None o' your fuckin' business!" shouted Marty. "Looks like you caught your partner's 'puttin'-his-nose-where-it don't-belong' disease, heh?"

"Calm down, Martin," said Milt.

"Don't you tell me to calm down, you mealy-mouthed appeaser, you!" he shouted before jumping back out of the car and walking, quickly and angrily, in the opposite direction down Bedford.

"What kind of walk is he walking now?" asked Tom.

"An anger walk," said Milt.

Before making an illegal U-turn so that he could bring his troubled partner back into their codependent fold, Milt said, "Marty got drunk that night and passed out and had a dream, and in that dream he had a twenty-foot dong which Martha Raye, with her larger-than-life mouth and what have you, gobbled every inch of like it was a cocktail frank. And so, when Marty woke up from the dream, he snuck into Martha's tent—he was still drunk, mind you—and kidnapped her and started dragging her by the loose skin on her back toward enemy lines, which he wanted to cross in order to get a German officer to marry them, bein' that no American officer would take on that kind of authority."

"What happened?" asked Tom, loving the show biz lore of it.

"Martha screamed, people came running, and Marty got busted down to E-1 and spent seven months in the brig with a colored guy who kept trying to teach him astral projection so's the two of 'em could get back to Philly, the guy's hometown, and wait the war out working in his old man's cheese steak shack. Cute story, eh?"

What had been done to Bob and Tom's minds and nervous systems over the past few hours made them unable to respond. Upset, on the one hand, by the thought that Milt and Marty—two guys that they were on the verge of looking up to but thank God hadn't started to yet because, naive as they were, they weren't that naive—might possibly be just a smidge on the unstable side, they were energized, on the other hand, by what each of them knew had been a free, no-holds-barred show biz—not to mention life—experience.

Because, regardless of the details—and people being dragged by their loose skin—"it's show biz," said Tom, "and hallelujah, brother, we are finally in it!"

MARTIN
GETS VISIONS

||||||||||||||||||||||||||||

B y the time Leopold and Sand returned to Paramount Studios that afternoon the enormity of the mistake they'd made had become crystal clear. By opting, on their first day in show business, to spend three hours away from the office as pawns in a Marty Sloyxne–orchestrated "worship gander" of Milton Berle's organ, which turned out to be not his organ at all, they'd destroyed whatever chance they might eventually have had to forge workable relationships with the other writers brought in to save the *Give Your Uncle Back His Legs* pilot.

Tom and Bob spent the rest of that afternoon sitting around the long table in the writers' room, observing, in stunned silence, as Norman Smalnitz oversaw his band of green-complected men in what he hoped would be "a session of free-flowing, free-form, fabulously fresh and funny story pitches, in case this pile of shit we're knocking our brains out on actually gets picked up." Leopold and Sand guessed that the median age of the older writers, whose credits had been available for reading on sitcom crawls since television's brown lipstick days, to be seventy-two, which also happened to be the approximate age of the stale recycled episode ideas they were now regurgitating into the flesh-pecking atmosphere of the room.

Somewhere deep within the third hour of their imprisonment, Marty Sloyxne jumped out of his chair and raced from the building shouting "Ray-Ray, wait for Daddy! Daddy's coming, Ray-Ray! Your daddy's on his way, my darling brown-eyed boy!"

"Ray-Ray," as explained to them by Milt Wagonman, was Marty's twenty-four-year-old son, Raymond Errol Flynn Sloyxne, who had been in a Glendale mental hospital since the age of twenty for stowing away in a storage room in the Hollywood Wax Museum before emerging to perpetrate an after-hours "sexual battery" on the Judy Garland statue "right there under the beautiful lights of the *Wizard of Oz* diorama."

According to Milt, "All's the kid said when the Hollywood dicks picked him up was, 'The Lion really is a coward! He didn't even try to stop me.'"

"And now we have to work with the crazy bastard who gave that crazy bastard life," said Manny Zolodny, the four-hundred-pound joke-smith whose major credit, to that point, had been writing "everything the one-toothed fuckin' dragon puppet ever said!" on *Kukla, Fran, and Ollie*.

Tom and Bob joined Milt and the other writers as they watched an emotionally distraught Marty stand outside their open window and try to talk his son into "lettin' me off the fuckin' guilt hook." The person to whom he was speaking, however, was not his son at all, but a sixty-four-year-old Native American extra he'd never met named—according to seventy-six-year-old writer-gossip Irv (I Know Something You Don't Know) Hienz—Joseph Glistening Hawk, who along with his jet-black-dyed and braided hair had recently completed three days' work as Cochise's blind medicine man on the *Bonanza* episode where Little Joe gives yellow fever to the Apaches.

When Tom and Bob asked Milt how his partner could possibly

have mistaken a sixty-four-year-old man for his twenty-four-year-old son, he shrugged and said, "Martin gets visions."

When the boys looked back out at Marty, he had Joseph Glistening Hawk in a vicious headlock and was shouting, "Wouldja forgive me, kid? Wouldja forgive me for bein' a bad father?"

Glistening Hawk, whose eyes betrayed the fact that he didn't know what the hell was going on except for the fact that his skull was being squeezed like a grape by an obvious madman, said, "Yes, I forgive you, I forgive you," which was nowhere near good enough for Marty.

"Say the whole fuckin' thing, my beloved boy!" he shouted, applying more pressure to the old man's head, at which point Milt, who'd obviously been in this kind of situation before, said to himself, "Okay, Milton. Looks like it's time for you to be getting your aging derriere out there."

Tom and Bob, and the other writers, followed on his heels, oblivious to Norman Smalnitz's "Where the fuck d'you red-assed monkeys think you're fuckin' goin'? I have a fuckin' show to get picked up for the fall, remember?"

The writers got outside just in time to hear Joseph Glistening Hawk tell Marty what he wanted to hear. "I forgive you for being a bad father, Daddy—"

"That ain't the whole thing!" said Marty. "Say the rest, like I tol' ya!"

"—and I love you very, very much. You are my role model!" said Glistening Hawk.

Marty smiled, released his victim from the headlock, stuck his hand in his own pocket, removed a dollar bill, folded it into Glistening Hawk's trembling right palm, closed the poor day player's fingers over the bill, mussed his hair, said, "Don't tell your mother," and sent him on his way to the makeup department. Then, Marty turned to Milt with a tear in his eye and said, "He forgave me, pally. He forgave me for bein' a bad daddy."

"That's wonderful, pally," said Milt, ushering Marty back toward their building the way James Brown's unnamed assistant always used to usher the be-caped Godfather of Soul back toward the mic after he'd been felled by one of his famously debilitating onstage soul-swoon spells.

Back in the office Milt helped Marty, who said he needed "just a battery-charging mini-nap," onto the couch in the tiny room euphemistically referred to as the writers' "lounge," and then rejoined the rest of the staff in the writers' room, where an extremely unhappy Norman Smalnitz was chastising everyone for jumping ship.

"Not once in all my years in this fuckin' business have I seen a less professional group of writers than all o' you!" he said. "To get up and walk out of this sacrosanct room because one of your fuckin' peers thinks an Indian is his son is pure minor fuckin' league! Marty Sloyxne–style nervous breakdowns are a dime a dozen in this fuckin' business, you sad, rubber-headed bunch of shriveled pricks, but a funny show is a rare treasure that can transform your lives from a garage apartment on La Brea with one of those half addresses to something you can actually invite people to!"

Smalnitz had not quite finished berating the writers, and Bob was not quite through trying to forget how the *Bonanza* medicine man reminded him of his father's wrestling persona, when the door opened and Marty entered, looked at Smalnitz, and said, in reference to the sheet of paper he was holding in his hand, "I didn't want the day to end without giving you this, Normie."

"What the fuck is it, Marty?" asked Smalnitz. "Your suicide note?"

"No," said Marty, ignoring the vicious little titters coming from eight of the eleven other old scribes. "It's a few ideas Milt and I came up with for your terrific new show that, please God, will run a hundred years."

Smalnitz grabbed the sheet from Marty's hand, glanced at it as though he knew how bad whatever he was about to read was going to be, then relaxed and said, "Well, whaddya know? It looks like Mr. Wagonman and Mr. Sloyxne have finally learned how to do it. Listen t' these excellent story ideas, gentlemen . . ."

It took Tom and Bob a few seconds to absorb the fact that what Smalnitz was reading had been written by them, Tom and Bob, on the previous night, during their too-excited-to-sleep show biz eve brainstorming marathon, and their reaction to the fact that Marty had, during his mini-nap, obviously broken into their belongings and stolen their ideas before presenting them as having been written by him and Milt affected them in slightly different ways.

Whereas Tom got so angry his sinus hurt, Bob wanted to hit Marty over the head with the big green whimsical "frog fishing with boy" lamp at the end of the filthy couch.

It felt like the end to Leopold and Sand, both as a writing team and as caring human beings. Marty Sloyxne had stolen their work and put his and his partner's name on it, and the producer—the boys' first producer ever!—had liked it, and praised Marty for it, and never once questioned whether or not he and his partner, who'd never written anything half as good, had actually written it!

Bob followed a furious Tom into the men's room, where Tom told him that, unless he agreed "to go back out there with me and tell Smalnitz what happened and get Marty's ass fired," he would go home and have an asthma attack and "*not* use my inhaler!" Fortunately, Bob was able to talk him down.

"Take a breath and relax, man," Bob kept saying. "It's part of the whole insane thing. This business is definitely full of assholes, but the only nonassholes who get ahead in it are the ones who don't let the more seasoned assholes get the best of them, and we shouldn't either, because we're good writers. Look how Smalnitz loved what we did, even if he doesn't know we did it."

"Where I come from," said Tom, "people give other people credit for the work they do."

"You come from the same Jersey City I do," Bob told him.

"Right," Tom said and smiled . . . a little bit.

"Where we come from, but mostly on the block where *I* came from"—Bob put his hand on his friend's shoulder—"life is worse than Hollywood. In my house, Marty would be a hero because he took care of himself, and that's what we have to do too."

"You call caving in and letting that dick steal our stuff 'taking care of ourselves'?" Tom, as angry as he was, thought he looked heavy in the bathroom mirror.

"Do you think Smalnitz really gives a crap who wrote it, Tommy? He's not a noble movie character, man. He's a schlemiel in his fifties who's holding on to the show biz ledge by his fingernails. Why do you think he teaches comedy at night school, because he's Mr. Chips? The man has had eleven failed pilots in a row. All he cares about is getting his latest turd on Monday nights at nine and keeping it there. Marty did us a favor. It's a test, man. We're being tested, okay? It's the 'Do you belong in show biz?' test, and if we leave we fail. Whaddya say? Do we run back home and get a real job and sit at desks at our little nine-to-fives for the rest of our lives or look back on what happened today as the disgraceful learning experience that it was?"

Before Tom could answer, Milt entered the men's room and said, "If you turn him in, boys, it'll kill him. Even though it would be the absolute right thing for you to do as people, it'd be the absolute most worst thing you could do to a Marty Sloyxne as individuals. The man is a lost dove floating above an . . . I don't know what. His life is falling apart. His sixth wife—the only one he ever truly loved and who ever got past his personality to truly love him, in this layman's opinion—just filed for a divorce three days ago and he feels ruined. The man cooks his dinner on a lightbulb. Stealing your work, as bad a thing to do as that was, was a compliment from one generation to the next. He would never steal ca-ca—only good stuff—and your material is some of the best he ever pretended came from him, and I mean that! Marty just read out loud to Norman and the other guys and it is terrific, and the reaction he got from Norman has given him, in that sweet sick mind of his, a new beginning. As hard as that may be for you guys to understand, it's the truth. It's four-twenty in the afternoon in the man's fifty-third year of life, but he feels, all of a sudden, like it's a new morning and he's a kid, and it doesn't burn when he pees, which is a feeling, I assure you, at three-twenty he did not feel."

Tom and Bob folded. And though they didn't turn Marty in they had grown a harder skin and learned a valuable lesson, which was, "Never again." Never again, they promised each other, would they let anyone screw them the way they'd been screwed by Marty Sloyxne.

They told Milt that they would let his partner get away with "artistic genocide" only if he sat down with them after work that day and focused on the meaning of their words when they told him that they knew what he did, and that if it ever happened again they would file a formal complaint against him with the Writers Guild. Milt, the ultimate enabler, tried to talk them out of that, too, but they stood firm.

Marty Sloyxne was already seated and chomping away at one of the three chili dogs before him when Leopold and Sand arrived at his table under the plastic rain canopy to the rear of Pink's Hot Dogs on La Brea.

"Guess who just left," he said through a pound of meat, bread, onions, and chili. "Marilyn Monroe! And she's still got the scrumptious dairy domes and the catch-me-kiss-me tucus on her, too. What a bona fide piece of barbiturate-loving American ass!" The boys pointed out that whomever he thought was Marilyn Monroe couldn't have been, since Ms. Monroe had been dead for several years.

"Bullshit!" screeched Marty, in a rare falsetto. "That's what they *want* you to believe!"

Although it was difficult to get back to the reason they'd asked Marty to meet with them, Tom and Bob eventually laid down the law to him, finishing with, "We mean it, Marty. Steal from us again and we'll turn you in." Raucous laughter was the last thing they expected from him, and the first thing they got.

"What's funny, Marty?"

"Funny, fellas? Nothin's funny. Try beautiful. Cuz that's what you guys are. You remind me of me so much when I was your age. I would stand up to people and I loved myself for it! So should you . . . pass the relish. Because the way I see you two wonderful guys is through the eyes of the father. Biology? I say biology can suck my dick! I say, regardless of the fact that you didn't begin your journey toward life inside my nuts, you two, because you confronted me, are as much my flesh and blood sons as your big brother Raymond. Far as I'm concerned, I am your daddy and here are the keys to the car! Oh, if you order the chili get it with cheese and I'll have a spoonful!"

In the car on the way back home that night Tom and Bob decided that Marty's eventual promise never to steal their work again was meaningless when compared to the larger issue—the thing about him being their "daddy." It creeped them out slightly, which, they decided, was a good thing, as it would—or so they thought—keep them forever aware of his every move.

Marty spent the rest of that week on *Give Your Uncle Back His*

Legs, pretending to be genuinely contrite about what he'd done to Tom and Bob, which, they knew, was as close as he could get to actually being contrite. He brought them their own separate editions of the *New York Times* each morning and left Hershey's Kisses and miniature Mounds and hard-boiled eggs on which he drew funny faces on their respective desks. To their credit, they didn't cave in and say "Thanks, Daddy!" which they knew, in their hearts, was what Marty wanted them to do. Unlike Milt and Marty, the other men on the staff were, as far as Tom and Bob could tell, fully formed human beings who, although their nastiness originated from a deep, poorly lit place within their souls, seemed capable of accepting amends from two other members of their species who, because they'd been young and naive, hadn't known the rules of the game.

The boys thought, quite naively, that their Marty Sloyxne problems were over and they could go back to kind of enjoying him when, in fact, their Marty shit storm was just gathering steam. He would show up at their apartment on Sycamore almost every night, always needing to "talk and share and vent and eat all over your couch," and he would proceed to ramble on for hours about the "deeply ruinous reem job" he called his life.

"I figured it all out," he kept saying. "If you had parents you're outa luck!"

The boys decided to find a new place to live as quickly as possible, without letting anyone in the office know their new address. Within an hour of their decision they were standing in the living room of the landlord's unit at the Silver Screen Cottages, a lovely pre–World War II Hollywood garden apartment complex belonging to Dot and Fern Shubert, who, in their vaudeville heyday, had been called the Whirling Shuberts and had worked with the likes of Cantor and Jessel, Benny and Tucker, and a young Jan Murray.

Fern Shubert told the boys that she and her sister rented only to show people, and then only if they got "the good feeling" about them. Fern told Tom and Bob that she and Dot got the good feeling about *them* because they knew, the minute they laid eyes on them, that they had "the funny." Dot told the boys that "the funny" oozed from their pores like "a bilge coolie's sweat" and that "you didn't have to do nothin' for us t' know you had it. You got the funny and we know it so welcome home!"

After being held in what felt like unusually desperate, long-lasting bear hugs by the two women, the team signed a one-year lease agreement, drank a celebratory champagne cocktail (the ShopRite generic brand, bottled in El Segundo, its $3.88 price sticker intact), and accepted, with make-believe enthusiasm, the Shubert sisters' invitation to them to attend the traditional Welcome New Tenants back-yard party in their honor on the following Saturday.

"D'ya like pulled pork?" asked Fern.

"She's talkin' about a possible menu item," said Dot. "Not your personal lives."

"My sister has the funny too," said Fern, who waited until Tom and Bob were finished pretending to laugh to say, "It'll be the best barbecue of your lives! As luck would have it, one of our other tenants is a genius of the form."

Back at work in the three days preceding their party, Marty badgered the boys incessantly about how they "could do this" to him. "You disappeared in the middle of the fuckin' night, fellas! D'ya think that's normal behavior for a person? What the fuck did you do that for without tellin' anybody where you were goin'? What? Y' tryin' t' ditch me or somethin'?"

Had they known that their yes would trigger in Marty a pathological obsession with them, with ramifications neither man nor science would ever fully comprehend, Tom and Bob probably wouldn't have said it—or at least said it separately.

The Saturday of the party was a beautiful Old Hollywood spring day, the kind of day it must have been when James Dean first hit town from Indiana. That was the way both of the boys still thought back then—even with their Marty torment, they were still addicted to the idea of Hollywood, and their imagined details of the lives of its iconic symbols still thrilled them. They were stirred from their first good night's sleep by the smell of Dot's braunschweiger, eggs, and coffee as it lifted them out of their beds the way it used to do to the silent, hapless, jug-eared traveling salesmen characters who floated in midair from their beds to Betty Boop's kitchen in the afternoon cartoons of their youth.

At six o'clock sharp the next day, the boys were escorted by Fern and Dot into their backyard, where a side of pork was already sizzling on the barby and where their new neighbors had already gathered. As they stood chatting with former Lawrence Welk Orchestra tenor saxophonist Walter ("Y' Wanna Know What That Cheap Polish Cock-wad Paid Me All Those Twenty-eight Years? A Hundred and Eighty-seven Dollars and Fifty Cents Per Show, Year After Fucking Year!") Olkiewicz, Dot walked up behind them and said, "Boys, I'd like you to meet the king of the Silver Screen Cottages barbecue . . . your newest neighbor in unit five, Marty 'The X Is Silent!' Sloyxne!"

Neither Tom nor Bob turned around.

"Hello, fellas," said Marty, stepping around to face them, a mad twinkle in his eyes and an equally loony grin on his face. "Looks to me like you can run but you can't hide, if ya follow what I'm sayin'." Then he laughed a laugh—a rumbling "B-waaaaaaaaaaaaa!" that ricocheted off the cheap North Hollywood walls—and Tom and Bob spent the rest of the party in their honor standing in numbed silence, responding monosyllabically when the other tenants introduced themselves, when Milt and his wife Gwen "World's Most Nervous Woman" Wagonman showed up, and when Marty whispered to them that the Shubert girls had been "quite wild, in the nymphomaniacal fornicative sense, in their day," but had "found the Lord" during "an intimate nine-hour bone-a-thon fivesome with Forrest Tucker, Scatman Crothers, and Francis the Talking Mule" in their dressing room at the old Baltimore Pantages. Marty, whose pulled pork was, as much as Tom and Bob hated to admit it, fabulously tangy, got the Shubert sisters drunk on his famous papaya daiquiris—the recipe for which he said he'd acquired from John Barrymore's personal abortionist—and eventually handed the barbecuing duties over to Milt and disappeared with "the old gals" into their unit, from which their screams eventually caused everyone to run to their aid. Marty, who had apparently tried to get them into bed—the disheveled, distraught late-middle-aged sisters were on their backs, dresses over their heads, on their living room floor, sobbing over the fact that their scrapbook, which had contained every clipping, every photo, every detail from their overlooked career, had been accidentally ripped in half by Marty's "ape paws"—dashed past Leopold and Sand with the Shuberts' TV in his arms, disappearing like a looter into the West Hollywood night as the boys and their neighbors tried to console the ex-vaudevillians.

"Our scrapbook," sobbed Fern.

"When we wouldn't pleasure him, he pleasured himself all over our beloved scrapbook," sobbed Dot.

Two policemen showed up and took a statement from the Shubert sisters, as well as witness statements from Leopold and Sand, whose jaws fell open when Marty, stolen TV set still in his arms, burst back into the apartment of the Shuberts, laughed uproariously, and, along with the policemen and the rest of the Silver Screen Cottages' tenants, pointed mocking index fingers at Tom and Bob, who'd been had.

"Holy shit, everybody!" shouted Marty to the sixty people crowded into the sisters' apartment. "Are our newest neighbors gullible or what! God, I love these guys!"

WHO IS THE MAN WHO RIDES THE SHARK? (SHARK RIDER IS HIS NAME-O)

||||||||||||||||||||||||||||

*G*ive Your Uncle Back His Legs proved, in the end, to be a victory for Tom and Bob when one of them—they never say which one wrote the line but both believed in his heart, at the time, that it was himself—came up with the show's biggest laugh line, which was "Look, Ma, no legs!" Although the line—which was spoken by actor and real-life amputee Duke McMasters, who played "Uncle Gus"— made the studio audience, which had been bused in from a pedophilia halfway house in Salinas, laugh harder than any other in the show it was cut from the edited air version because Norman Smalnitz immediately caved in to the network when one of its censors decided the dialogue was "coarse and unrefined." Although the line was killed, Marty took credit for it anyway, insisting that he had pitched it "two minutes before the big-headed kid or the skinny kid who won't eat pitched it, but nobody heard me 'cause I had phlegm in my throat."

When he asked Milt for confirmation—"You heard me pitch it first, right, Milty?"—Milt said that he'd heard all of Marty's phlegm "but I can't in all honesty say that I heard you say the line." Marty, who was incensed by what he perceived as his partner's betrayal, told everyone in the writers' room, including the nineteen-year-old writer's assistant, that Milt had been a bedwetter "through high school" and that his mother had forced him to wear his urine-stained mattress cover when he went trick-or-treating on Halloween night 1921.

After the pilot wrapped, Tom and Bob were approached by an agent named Todd Berkoborowitz, who had been in the studio audience during the taping and had made his highly focused way through a crowd of depressed creatives in search of "whoever the fuck it was who came up with the brilliant 'Look, Ma, no legs!'" When Berkoborowitz found Tom and Bob the first words out of his mouth were "My name is Todd, and I'm the best agent in town, and I want you to know that if you're the guys who wrote 'Look, Ma, no legs,' then I'm the guy who *might* consider representing you. Are you interested in my considering it?"

"God, yes!" said Tom.

"Please God, yes!" said Bob.

"Gentlemen," said a suddenly even more arrogant Berkoborowitz, "one good line on the worst pilot ever created does not a career make. We should meet, talk, and watch each other eat over some let's-get-acquainted egg whites tomorrow morning" at Sambo's flagship restaurant on La Cienega Boulevard.

Young Turk killer agent Berkoborowitz was quick to pick up on all the excited, nervous energy pissing Tom and Bob off at each other as they joined him in his reserved window booth at Sambo's the next day.

"What do you want, boys?" he asked.

"Umm," said Tom. "Maybe I'll take a quick gander at the menu first and see what kind of fruit they have, if any—"

"I'll have a sausage and cheddar omelet with home fries," said Bob, as though trying to impress Berkoborowitz with how sure he was about what he wanted.

"I mean out of your careers," said Berkoborowitz.

"Oh," said Bob.

"I knew that was what he meant," lied Tom.

"If you knew it was what he meant," retorted Bob, "why did you go into the fruit soliloquy from the play 'Oh, How I Want This Guy to Sign Me'?"

"Shut up," said Tom.

"You shut up," said Bob.

"Both of you shut up," said Berkoborowitz. "I want you to shake hands and forgive each other for whatever the fuck it is that's ruining our first career strategizing breakfast together."

Though they'd always envisioned that their perfect surrogate father would turn out to be someone older than them, Tom and Bob were thrilled at the young man's focus.

"Life is short, boys," said Berkoborowitz. "I could walk outside right now and get hit by the bus you two guys didn't want me to see you step off of, so let's talk business before the seventy-year-old waitress shows up with her little pad and unfulfilled life. So, again, I ask you. What is it you *want*?"

"I want to do good work," said Tom.

"Me, too," said Bob.

"Something on the level of *The Honeymooners* or *The Dick Van Dyke Show*."

"I'm right there with you," said Bob. "I'd like for us to be remembered as two of the best comedy writers of all time."

"I'd be happy to be remembered as *among* the two very best," said Tom.

"Me, too," said Bob. "'Among' would be fine."

"'Among' would be completely better, actually!" Both writers were concerned now with how conceited they might possibly have come across.

"How 'bout money?" asked Berkoborowitz.

"Money?" Tom said with the exact inflection Todd had used.

"Is it important to you? Because it's important to me."

"It's important to me, too," said Tom. "Very important."

"It's very, very important to me," said Bob.

"Is it 'very, very' important to you, Tom?" asked Berkoborowitz.

"I grew up with money so it's even *more* important to me!" said Tom.

"In that case," said Berkoborowitz, pausing for affect, "I . . . will . . . be . . . your . . . agent."

Todd Berkoborowitz would guide an overly grateful Leopold and Sand toward viable comedy writing team status, securing them work on shows that ran the entire gamut of mediocrity—shows such as *Phish Out of Water* and *Mr. and Mrs. Abominable Snowman* and *Three Little Pigs*, which was about slovenly college freshmen triplet sisters who room together at an unnamed east coast university.

And as Tom and Bob's success grew Milt and Marty's—but especially Marty's—envy toward them also grew and festered.

"They're like everyone else in this fuckin' town," said Marty, as he and Milt read the *Variety* blurb announcing that Leopold and Sand, whom they'd so lovingly guided through their first shaky day in the entertainment industry, had been named story editors on *Three Little Pigs*. "By which I mean they're ungrateful *shit asses*!"

Milt and Marty were in the Hollywood failed writers' tavern the Cyclops at the moment they read *Variety*'s heralding of Leopold and Sand's promotion. The fact that the joint was full of people—mainly

Milt & Marty

Samoan tourists straight off the "See Hollywood" Gray Line bus—only added fuel to Marty's rage. And how could it not? For here were two men (one always much angrier than the other), staring old age in the puss, still being forced by circumstance to get free shoes once a year at the Writers Guild thrift store. One year things were so bad that Milt had to wear white nurse's shoes polished brown to meet 'n' greets with network executives young enough to be his sperm.

"Leopold and Sand are like everyone else in this fuckin' town—ungrateful!" Marty hissed at Milt for the second time in a minute. "We suckled those two helpless little boy-bitch embryos, who couldn't even tie their own shoes with a joke, and put them under our wings! We protected 'em from Smalnitz and the rest of those vultures who wanted their sweet blood of youth! We got them through their hazardous initiation period unscathed! We showed them *Milton Berle's cock* for godsakes!"

Milt half-whispered that, in fact, they had not even been able to show Tom and Bob baseball great Roy Campanella's penis.

"We didn't *have* to show them *anybody's* penis!" Marty whelped so loudly that a woman at the end of the bar shot him a dirty look. Marty replied to the woman's slight by opening his shirt and showing her his heart surgery scar. "Wanna talk about courage for a moment, lady? Because I have to shit through my *heart*! Okay? So maybe . . . just *maybe* that entitles me to say the word 'penis' above a whisper!" Chastened, the woman went back to her brandy alexander. "Women!" Marty snarled. "One vagina and they think they're Queen Turd of Shit Island!"

Milt wondered aloud, since it was dinnertime, if he shouldn't call his beloved Gwen and tell her he might be late for supper. Marty told him to stop thinking of his wife for one goddamn minute, "you pussy-whipped half homo, and focus on our *careers*! We're gonna be in a twelve-dollar pine box in two minutes, for crissakes!"

"What does the success of two nice young fellas have to do with *our* careers, Martin?" Milt really wanted to know, he wasn't just playing devil's advocate.

"You don't get it, do you, Milt? You've been rubbing the lamp of my joke-genie for forty years and you still don't understand the power of hate!"

Milt, hurt by the remark, said that he understood part of the power of hate very well. Marty put him on the spot by asking which part of the power of hate he understood. Milt hesitated, then told Marty that he didn't *have* to tell him which part of hate he understood but "let's just say it's the best part, and let it go at that." That stopped Marty in his tracks. "Okay, so you understand the power of hate. I'll stick a rocket in my ass and fire it over the Boston harbor!"

Marty tried to enjoy his whiskey and Ovaltine but the jealous poison resurfaced. "I hate those two ungrateful fucks, because I'll tell you something, Milton, and I say this with love, until you can hate as deep as me the people who get ahead of you in life through no fault of their own, then you'll never have the fire in your belly to live in anything better than a wetback's garage!"

"My house isn't a wetback's garage."

Marty told Milt that he didn't mean it literally but was insulting his home to make a "bigger" point.

"Oh," Milt said, soothed.

"God, I hate Tom and Bob . . . I just hate 'em like . . . I used to hate Nikita Khrushchev." Swayed somewhat now by the sheer weight of Marty's hate, Milt had to agree that Tom and Bob weren't "all *that* much more talented than us."

"Now you're seeing the light," Marty said, rubbing Milt's head like it was 1930 and Milt was a shoeshine boy outside Pennsylvania Station.

"And what do they do when they start getting hot?" Marty, no longer happy with raging to Milt alone, asked Cora, the fifty-four-year-old bartender-owner of the Cyclops, who happened to have been born with both eyes in one socket, which happened, it was said, to have been driven to the center of her head by corrective retina surgey gone horribly wrong. "They fuckin' forget us!"

"No good deed ever goes unpunished, Marty," said Cora. Cora had always had a thing for Marty, and he for her. Her being an actual cyclops made him desire her sexually in the worst way, but the bar was one of the few places on earth Marty felt comfortable, and he didn't want to fuck up his welcome there on the slight chance the affair went south.

"I wanna do them little pricks some real, bona fide harm," said Marty to Milt, after Cora turned to another customer and after he imagined taking the barmaid from behind late one night after the bar closed, riding the mechanical bull together, naked, while he shouted at the top of his lungs, "Blink your one eye for me, baby! Blink it hard for Marty!" Marty got his mind off the pleasures of the flesh and back on to business.

"I want to do them little pricks some harm . . . Did I say that already?" Marty asked Milt, who was now lost in a daydream of his own. This was a Wednesday night, and Gwen always made meat loaf on Wednesdays. He loved his wife's meat loaf as much as he loved the dear woman herself. She put pimientos in it for him and made the top of it crusty, the way he liked it, with Campbell's tomato soup baked right in.

His revelry was ruptured by the poking of Marty's left index finger.

Marty told Milt to get his mind onto something positive. Milt then looked around the joint for something positive, gave up, and just started watching the TV hanging by a filthy chain over the bar, at which point he shouted, "Look, Martin! Sharks! Your favorite!"

Sure enough Marty looked up at the screen and saw a PBS nature documentary on the great white shark, which prompted him to start soliloquizing, in his now drunken state, having knocked back the drinks of nearby customers when they weren't looking, about "this new idea I just got in my head . . . It's about a private eye, name of Johnny Mako, who rides a fuckin' shark along the Venice–Santa Monica–Malibu coast solvin' crime! And you know what we're gonna call it? *Shark Rider*!"

Milt had witnessed this before. He had seen his partner get blessed with a thunderbolt of creativity a few times before and it excited the hell out of him. Milton Abraham Lincoln Wagonman forgot all about meat loaf.

"Go, Marty! Go, Marty!" Milt cheered, feeling a bit like Vincent van Gogh's friends must have felt—if the poor crazy bastard had had any friends—after Vincent chose to use a yellow-colored paint nobody'd ever dreamed of using before . . . or when whoever the hell it was broke the sound barrier or some such thing.

Marty was getting that same genius look in his eyes he'd gotten the other two times he struck creative gold. He had that look when he thought up their never produced pilot *My Mother the Chihuahua*, about a mama's boy whose mother dies and comes back as the smallest dog in the world; or the failed spec *To Gnome Him Is to Love Him*, about a troll who gets a job writing a lovelorn column. And eureka! Marty had that look again now!

"Yeah, Johnny Mako . . ." Marty was off his stool now pacing the bar. "The Shark Rider could ride his shark for justice and to clear his name for some crime. We'll never say *which* crime, so we don't alienate the audience.

"Who is the man who rides the shark?"

Even Marty's improvised song was close to being in tune.

"Shark Rider is his name-O. Riding sharks to clear his name from a crime for which he was framed-O!"

Milt felt it was time to do what *he* did for the partnership, i.e., mold and sculpt the genius of Marty's original concept. "What if, Marty . . . and I'm just spitballing now . . ."

"Spitball, Milton! Spitball for the love of holy God!" Marty was excited too. This felt good, this felt *right*!

"Well, what if we don't call the lead 'Johnny Mako' but we call him 'John Sharkrider' and it's just a coincidence that he rides a shark. Like if you had a show called *Murphy's Law* and the guy jus' happened to be called Murphyslaw and he jus' happened to be a lawyer?"

Marty thought for a long time. "I like it," he said in a quiet almost biblical voice.

The excited comedy vets left the Cyclops and repaired to Milt's little house in Sherman Oaks, which Milt and his wife shared with Gwen's mother, Gladys, age 109. The old lady's claim to fame, and one that made her feel superior to every other human being she had ever come into contact with, was the "historically true" fact that she had been in Ford's Theater the night President Abraham Lincoln had been shot. (It was for this reason, days after first meeting Gwen, that Milt legally changed his middle name from Pinyik to Abraham Lincoln.) She was just a little girl of seven at the time, and her parents had promised her "a comedy" for her birthday. *Our American Cousin* was playing at Ford's and Gladys still owned the little pinafore she had been wearing when John Wilkes Booth jumped out of the presidential box and onto the stage, sending a plume of assassin sweat upon her frock. To be honest, the mean little woman had always felt worse about her dress than about the death of Honest Abe. That's the kind of woman she was. Gwen's ancient mother had held it over her and Milt's heads that she owned this valuable piece of American history, and that she might sell it someday to a museum so her daughter and son-in-law could escape their crushing debt, but . . . then again . . . she might *not.* Milt, who could never hate anyone, hated his mother-in-law but what could he do? She was his dear, sainted wife's mother and, besides, she held the note on the house.

Gwen, who was thrilled by Milt's excitement over the new project, made a big pot of coffee and got out the comedy team's legal pad so they could jot down and not lose any of the gold. Marty stole some of Gladys's pain medication and settled down to work. It all came so easy—the great ideas always do! It was maybe the greatest creative roll Wagonman and Sloyxne had ever been on, and before they knew it ol' Mr. Dawn had snuck his red ass into the sky, leaving a legal pad with almost two full pages of dynamite ideas in it. Marty was too excited to go home to bed, so he stopped off at every motel pool on the drive home and swam one lap in each in his underpants. When he awoke later, his red hair was a pale green from the chlorine but he didn't care.

Three weeks later—or four times faster than it had ever taken them before—Milt and Marty were able to hold in their hands the most perfectly crafted spec pilot script since 1951, when they wrote *Golden American Finch,* which concerned an albino mail carrier from Lebanon, Illinois, who, after falling off the roof and landing on his head, discovers he has the ability to fly. They could hardly wait to put it into the hands of their sixty-pound, eighty-five-year-old agent, Bethany Mezner Roneth-Uffga, who had been representing the team since December 8, 1941. Bethany's opinion meant the world to Milt and Marty, so when they handed her the script at the Villa Veersailla-bella Retirement/Assisted Living (with a crematorium on the property) Hideaway, they held their breath.

"Guys . . . " Beth finally wheezed before lighting a Camel just under her emphysema oxygen tube that resided permanently now in her nostrils. "I think I can do something with this."

Three weeks after reading the *Shark Rider* script Bethany got her boys a deal to produce the pilot. And three weeks after that, CBS ordered a full season—twenty-two episodes—of the first series Wagonman and Sloyxne had ever created, written, and, most important, gotten on the air.

One of their first orders of business, after their respective euphorias had worn off, was to sit down together and build a writing staff.

The first three words out of Marty's mouth after Milt asked him, "So? Any ideas?" were "Leopold and Sand."

Milt was taken aback at first, what with Marty hating the younger men's guts and everything.

"I beg your pardon?" said Milt.

"You just don't get it, do you, Milton? I love those little shmendricks! Do you really think I could possibly hate their fucking guts this much if I didn't?"

When Wagonman and Sloyxne offered Leopold and Sand the "coproducers" credit on *Shark Rider*, the two younger men were torn. While the credit would signify a major career leap for them, they felt an apprehension that would have been natural for anyone who had ever been hammered in the figurative ass by an old man named Sloyxne. On the other hand, a credit with the word "producer" in it was something that every writer dreamed of achieving, for it held the key to many theretofore seemingly unattainable things, one of the most thrilling being a future. The boys stayed on the fence until Todd Berkoborowitz called them with the numbers—the money that Milt and Marty had said they would be willing to pay—at which point Tom and Bob gave Todd the green light to close the deal. With the money from *Shark Rider*, the boys would each be able to buy his own house and, per the American dream, when someone is able to buy a house in America, other amazing things—like a woman to love—might suddenly be more attainable.

"Methinks this might be grown-up time," said Bob, holding up a half-full glass of Fresca at his and Tom's celebratory Farmers Market lunch.

"Methinks you may be right, my liege," added Tom, clinking his partner's glass. "It might very well be time to trade in our binkies for BMWs."

For more than three seasons, life and work on *Shark Rider* went surprisingly well for the teams of Wagonman and Sloyxne and Leopold and Sand. Marty, who was distracted by the sudden awesome responsibilities he and Milt had been given, was much too busy to behave in a psychotic manner. Neck deep in the details of being one of the bosses of a show—running the writers' room, casting and editing each episode, overseeing wardrobe, hiring, firing, and maintaining staff morale, pleasing the network, and many other things—he was approaching, for the first time in his life, menschdom. And he was thriving in the role.

And Milt—not to mention his beloved Gwen, who was looking forward to moving from her mother's teeny-weeny Sherman Oaks house into a sprawling Beverly Hills north-of-Wilshire home of her own—couldn't have been happier.

As for Tom and Bob, they were learning more, and being given more responsibility (casting, costume, and lighting decisions), than ever before and the network, which was pleased with them, was eager to "go into business" with them—meaning that they were being looked at, all of a sudden, as potential show runners of the future. The fact that Tom and Bob were on the fast track toward getting their own series on the air, combined with the fact that Milt and Marty were, for the first time ever in their careers, getting the best tables at the best restaurants (Marty would even hold himself back from licking the bread until a basket of it arrived at his table) because they were at the helm of a show that was getting impressive ratings and building an audience every week, was making the four writers the definition of Hollywood success.

Milt and Marty were actually functioning happily—approaching a point where they had nearly paid off all the hideous debts each had incurred over the long course of their previously unsuccessful lives, while fulfilling their own fantasies about who they wanted to be. And that was when the bottom fell out of their little paradise. For that was when Marty, who was enjoying a serene Saturday morning stroll through downtown Olvera Street before driving over to the lot to put some finishing editing touches on *Shark Rider* episode #62, met an extraordinarily plain, deeply mystical, highly mysterious, seriously spiritual, truly fucking crazy woman named Choochy, thirty-plus years his junior, who, from her perch in her grandfather's Olvera Street glass-blowing stall, blew glass with lips so thin they never chapped. And it was through those lips that she shared with Marty, soon after he'd revealed to her that he was the "kingpin" on the *Shark Rider* television series, her deeply held belief that sharks did not really exist.

"Huh?" said Marty, sitting across from her at the taquito stand near her place of work, trying to figure out how he might get her to look upon his penis as a shapeless glob of molten, ready-to-be-blown glass.

"They don't exist, Martino!" the nearly lipless Latina said, dipping the end of a taquito into guacamole before sliding its green, slimy essence through her chap-free lips and into her workaday, pink mouth.

"There's no such thing as them. Sharks don't exist. The Gringo invented the shark to make people of color be afraid to swim in the ocean. That's it, plain and simple."

"Wow," said Marty.

"Wow, what?" she said. "Wow you think I'm a crazy Latina bitch?"

"No, my saint," Marty said, his world stopping on a dime. "Wow I think you're the first person I ever met who believes exactly as I have always believed, but never had the—how do you say it?—*cojones* to say out loud. Because I, too, have always believed that sharks were a myth, that they only existed so Jacques Cousteau could have a TV show, a belief I will hold, along with my hate of the Gringo, until the dying breath!"

Even though the last thing Marty said was a euphemism for "I want to get into your pants with all my cock," it impressed Choochy enough to let him lie on top of her, fully clothed, in a lightly frequented nearby alley.

On the following Monday morning Marty, with Milt and their writing and production staff gathered in his office, made a speakerphone call to the network and announced that there would be "a significant change" to *Shark Rider* after the episode that was scheduled to be shot that week—episode #63—was completed.

"Okay," said the happy voice of Aaron Prince, the young Harvard-educated executive whom CBS had assigned to "cover" *Shark Rider*. "We're all ears over here. Ready when you are, M. 'The X Is Silent!' S."

"Starting with episode sixty-four," said Marty, "all remaining episodes for the entire duration of the show will be written to accommodate the great and profound truth that sharks do not exist."

The sound of Prince's laughter, followed by the sound of the laughter of his three even younger underlings, who made their boss's satisfaction their only reason for being, arose from Marty's speakerphone.

"This is no joke, Aaron," Marty told him. "We're dead serious over here. Sharks don't exist, and *Shark Rider* will no longer be in the business of perpetrating the myth that they do."

"But Martin," said Prince, "you're just three episodes away from number sixty-six, which, as I'm sure you know, is the magic number for all show creators. The number after which, in terms of syndication monies, hit show creators never have to work again, should that be their life decision."

"The network has heard my decision," said Marty.

"And how does your partner feel about your decision?"

"My partner is my partner, Aaron, not because he and I feel differently about things but because we are of one mind on all things . . . on earth *and* under the sea!"

Had the emotionally shattered, furious Milt not been dry-heaving into a *Shark Rider* waste basket in the corner of the room at that moment, he might very well have had something to say that didn't jibe with Marty's opinion. All he could do, besides spew a heartsick vapor into the basket, was think to himself, over and over, *We were just three lousy doggoned episodes away from a life of wealth and leisure and he pulls this!*

The network, which was stuck with a hit series that was a near national sensation, à la *The Man from Uncle* or *The Partridge Family*, with toys and games and *Shark Rider* Big Wheel bikes, a line of children's clothing, decals that glowed in the ocean, lunch boxes with John Sharkrider waving from the thermos with Bullet his trusty shark, and a multitude of other *SR*-related products, dispatched a representative to the lot to have a "conversation" with Tom and Bob, in which Tom and Bob would be asked to act, for want of a better word, as spies who would keep the network informed about everything that Milt and Marty were thinking, with the unspoken implication being that after Milt and Marty were fired—as they would be, according to the representative, "as soon as the legal pishposh can be ironed out"—Tom and Bob would be elevated from their current co-producers status to that of co–executive producers.

"If it was up to me," said the representative, "I would pull the plug on those two crazy old delusional bastards and install you in their back-saving, two-thousand-dollar chairs right now!"

Tom and Bob were torn—thrilled, on the one hand, that they might soon be living their dream lives, with all of the attendant power and prestige, not to mention money, that came with it, and concerned on the other hand that they might very well not get to profit from a few more years of critical show biz seasoning before being drawn into one of the biz's—not to mention life's—ugliest events, i.e., "When the Mentees Pass the Mentors Right On By." Throwing their behavioral gear sticks into "R"—for Rationalization—they comforted themselves by reminding each other that Milt and Marty were never actually their mentors . . . that they were two probably decent but definitely troubled men into whom the two of them just happened to bump on their very first day in the show business capital.

Later that day, however—even before Tom and Bob were forced to sell their souls and begin to spy on Milt and Marty in a way that may or may not have made them feel dirty—Milt and Marty were replaced on *Shark Rider* by "the two Buddys," Jeff Buddy Issac and Bernie Buddy Steiff, who had, for many years, been stepping in and "saving" troubled sitcoms. And nowhere, to Tom and Bob's shock and dismay, was their supposed champion—the lowly network representative who'd come and presented to them the details of the plot against their bosses—to be found. And nowhere to be found either, there in the new land they and the other writers had just started to call Buddyville, was there any mention of naming them "co–executive producers." In fact, they were fired three days after the Great Buddy and Buddy Takeover because, as their agent Todd Berkoborowitz informed them over the phone, after telling them to "please keep your panic level down because I have acid reflux, and I need to say what I have to say and get to a bland lunch," their new bosses "Buddy and Buddy have decided to start fresh . . . bring in their own guys, and make *Shark Rider* their home away from home, which is their right. It's not personal," he said. "It's show biz."

Milt & Marty

With part of the $28 million they split after *Shark Rider* went into syndication, the two Buddys bought connecting 7,200-square-foot homes in Aspen, Colorado. With part of the $0 that Milt and Marty shared after the Writers Guild, for the first time in its history, gave Buddy and Buddy the never-before-used credit of "series re-creators," they bought nothing. Not that they didn't go to war with the network in a protracted court battle, but their choice of an attorney, as with their choice of almost everything else in their lives, proved less than wise.

Charles J. Nindle Jr. Esq's only big courtroom "rainmaker," as lawyers call a big payday, was winning a not guilty verdict for Dr. Singh Demos—or Doctor D, as he was called—who was a non–board certified plastic surgeon who became a millionaire in the sixties by performing face-lifts out of his van.

Gwen Wagonman demanded, shortly after Milt and Marty had lost all rights to *Shark Rider*, that Milt stay away from Marty, claiming that the man had been "nothing but poison to us from the very beginning!" Milt struggled to counter his wife's argument, pointing out to her that time on their honeymoon when Marty had sent a box of Omaha steaks to their Glendale motel room.

Gwen had every right to be angry, and Milt knew it. If Marty had only pretended to believe in the existence of sharks they would all have been on easy street. Maybe the woman was right. Maybe Martin Sloyxne wasn't the comedy deity Milt thought he was. Although it killed him to do it, Milt somehow found the strength to stay away from his partner . . . for almost a week. Finally, unable to bear the separation any longer, he hopped in his car late one night and drove down Hollywood Boulevard to try and catch a glimpse of Marty at his apartment window above Musso's. And it worked. There he was, Marty Sloyxne, standing at the window wearing only the top of his *Shark Rider* pajamas and staring out blankly at nothing. Or was Marty, Milt wondered, staring out at what might have been?

THE MIRRORING CURE

||||||||||||||||||||||||||

A s if Tom and Bob's confidence hadn't been shattered enough after being lied to by the network and then shit-canned by the two Buddys, Todd Berkoborowitz, the agent who had pledged to "go to the mat" for the guys, suddenly became too busy to take their calls. Todd's assistant Bram Sheisessen got "that tone" in his voice when the boys called—that future young, haughty Turk tone that says to the client, "I'm only answering phones now so that in a year I can be a harder-assed agent than the guy whose bottled water I'm fetching, so you'd better kiss my ass at the beginning of this process, or I swear that when I'm packaging shows I'll leave you so far out in the cold your balls will be a bluer blue than the Pacific Design Center!"

Even back when things were going well, Tom and Bob had made a point of being polite to Bram—it was just how they were raised—but now, with no show to work on, they began toadying up to him to such a degree that they pretended to be pleased when he detoured their phone calls to Zvi Rufkite, an entirely new baby agent-in-training, a fresh-out-of-the-mailroom wunderkind who was now being groomed by Todd Berkoborowitz to give the faltering careers of Leopold and Sand "your most minimal attention." Tom and Bob chose to believe that their demotion to Zvi's client list was, in some through the looking glass show biz kind of way, additional evidence of how much Todd cared about the trajectory of their careers, as opposed to what it really was, which was Todd's loss of confidence in their talent, which had been triggered by the Buddys having no confidence in their talent. Still, this new guy Zvi really seemed to care about Tom and Bob, almost as much as Todd had, three months earlier, when they were considered to be one of the hottest writing teams in town and Todd wanted to take vacations with them. (Tom had even bought a non-allergenic flowered shirt for a planned Hawaii trip.)

Zvi, who was still too young to know what "minimal attention" meant, hustled and got Tom and Bob back into the marketplace in a big way, using up a favor owed to him by an executive from another network who had, in a previous life, been the dealer from whom Zvi had purchased recreational pain medication. In gratitude to Zvi for having helped provide his daughter with a college education, the v.p. of comedy/drug dealer gave Tom and Bob the green light on a spec pilot of theirs called *Wright for Each Other. Wright,* as the country would so lovingly come to abbreviate the show, was about two distant cousins of Orville and Wilbur Wright, the fathers of flight—a funny, sexy ingenue and a handsome young lead actor, who Tom and Bob envisioned sparring their way through a Tracy and Hepburn or Sam and Diane–like relationship. Each week, he—a jockish satyr of a pilot for a commercial airliner—and she—a brainy, beautiful, independent feminist of a flight attendant—would pretend, while hurtling through the atmosphere at thirty thousand feet, not to be attracted to each other while a hefty percentage of the TV demographic would, it was hoped, know better and hardly be able to wait and see when the two characters "would bang each other," as Tom felt confident enough to put it during his and Bob's initial network pitch meeting.

A hit show is all about the casting. A great script with a bad cast will die on its feet. But a great cast with a half-assed script is almost certainly a lock for the Museum of Broadcasting. And so the latter was true for Tom and Bob. They had, in fact, written a much better pilot that was never produced and one that couldn't be cast because, during pilot season, there is a feeding frenzy caused by the fact that all the really good actors either have already committed to television projects or are starring in movies that are doing just well enough for the stars not to settle for television. But this time, for the team of Leopold and Sand, it all came together.

Jill Lumb, who was to play Lara in *Wright*, was fresh from an off-Broadway show called *Tell Mama I Saw a Naked Man's Ass*. A funny, vivacious woman of twenty-three, Jill was already considered "the fag hag to watch" in New York City. She was cute, handled comedy beautifully, and gave the strong impression of being terrified of men—qualities that made her perfect for the small screen.

Ty Carpenter, who was cast opposite her as Bud Carter, hadn't started out to be an actor at all. Ty had wanted to be a professional baseball player and had made it all the way to Triple-A before a scout for a local community theater spotted him and cast him as Joe in *Damn Yankees*, the musical about the baseball player who sells his soul to the devil. Ty, who never thought he'd love anything more than baseball but found during the course of his performance as Joe that he loved playing "moments" as an actor even more, moved to LA and committed himself to doing "only really good work." It was in LA, on just his fifth cattle call audition, where a casting director, whom everyone thought had been cured of his homosexuality by electric shock treatments, fell in even deeper, more instantaneous love with Ty than had the community theater scout who'd discovered him for *Damn Yankees*. Within a week Ty was reading in front of Tom and Bob for the male lead in *Wright for Each Other* and was offered the part on the spot. During the early stages of production, as kind of a kiss-up to the agent who'd "gotten us here," Tom and Bob named the pilot's male lead for their agent Zvi, which they changed to Bud when the network people said they found "Zvi" to be "too urban."

The chemistry between Lumb and Carpenter was palpable. Tom and Bob wondered, given the chops they'd acquired running a successful show, what would have happened if they had gotten their dream cast of the then unknown John Leguizamo and singer-songwriter Tracy Chapman for the roles of Lara and Bud. Bob had been so moved by a Chapman concert that he had her in to read for the network, where she proved to be not quite as funny as people had every right to imagine she would be. Leguizamo, on the other hand, was approved instantly by the executives but balked when they wouldn't guarantee that at least 50 percent of the writing staff be made up of Latino street comics.

When things go right in show business, they go right with an inevitability bordering on the preordained, as opposed to the other 98 percent of the time, when things go wrong with an irrefutable logic that seems much more preordained. Case in point? Just how easily the lovable supporting cast fell together on *Wright for Each Other*. To play Ruben, Bud's on again, off again alcoholic copilot, Mike "Tug" Andrews got up out of a hospital bed after a kidney transplant and "inhabited" the role. Andrews, a "real life" alcoholic, was nicknamed Tug because he wore a toupee no one was allowed to acknowledge, and he brought a tender, sympathetic insight to the role, making his catchphrase "I'm drunk, where's my airplane?" one that was repeated nationally around office water coolers.

For the role of Sally, the man-hungry, monkey-faced second banana, they had the great good fortune to bring Lucy Delle'bate out of retirement. Lucy had spent eight years in a convent after a painful divorce had left her without the sense of smell. Always in demand by the sitcom world as "our generation's Vivian Vance," Lucy was constantly wooed by producers during the entire time she spent with the Sisters of Montauk. One producer grew so desperate for a supporting player for his show that he bought the land out from under Lucy's nunnery, hoping that if the sisters were forced to do their good works and bake their bread in a half-abandoned mini-mall Delle'bate would "come to her senses" and return to television. The producer's plan worked beautifully.

Wright, which was touted by the network as "*Cheers* on an airplane," became a respectable if not a runaway hit, due in part to the lucky scheduling break it received when it debuted behind a juggernaut of a hit called *Juggernaut*.

Not only did the sudden, middle-of-the-road success of the show do wonders for Tom and Bob's standing in the business, and make them wealthy enough to have a battery of accountants who shared the first name Jerry, it had another, unforeseen, equally serendipitous result. Todd Berkoborowitz, who had left William Morris to start Berkoborowitz Partners Ltd., wooed the team away from Zvi Rufkite and the Morris agency with a promise to do even more for their careers than he'd promised them before dumping them off to the underling of an underling. Zvi didn't take Leopold and Sand's jumping ship lightly, however. He knew that Todd did a lot of blow—he had even stolen some of it during one of Berkoborowitz's famous New Year's Eve orgy-slash-Chinese cooking demonstrations—and he threatened to go public with what he knew unless Tom and Bob promised Zvi 5 percent of any of their future earnings. This was the kind of fight Todd Berkoborowitz lived for, though. And so he had Zvi beaten nearly to death by a deep tissue masseuse, which forced the younger, now fron-tal lobe–damaged agent to back off. Tom and Bob never heard about the beating, although they both raved about how good the masseuse was. If they had heard there is no doubt they would have left Todd and returned to Zvi, but they are pretty sure they never did hear about it. They did hear a little about it, but not so much that they believed any of what they'd heard. Well, they believed some of it, but such an infinitesimal amount that they were certainly not going to leave Todd on the strength of a rumor that had nothing more convincing than "the ring of truth" to it.

Over in Realityville, the sad suburb where Milt and Marty's careers had purchased cheap real estate years before, things were grim. Gwen Wagonman, who, rightly or wrongly, but mostly rightly, blamed Marty Sloyxne for the death of her dreams, threatened to leave Milt if he did not join her in "regular, long-term, deep, embarrassing, and emotion-ally painful" psychotherapy. Gwen also wanted what was left of her beloved husband out of show business, which, she said, "you never belonged in, not even for the lousy five minutes you were making a liv-ing in it!" It wasn't like Gwen to say hurtful things but the woman was hurting and "that's usually when the hurtful things get said," Milt whis-pered after locking himself in the toilet to have a good cry. Gwen, who heard her husband's whimpering through the door, asked Milt what was wrong. Milt responded, in an attempt to be brave, that he was cry-ing only because his prostate had grown to the size of a casaba melon and it hurt him to "go sissy." Gwen believed—or chose to believe—her man, and life, for the moment, went on.

If there were two thoughts Milt Wagonman never allowed himself to have they are these: (1) that something terrible might, God forbid, happen to Randi, the lesbian daughter who hadn't spoken to him and Gwen in thirty-five years, and (2) that he might someday be forced to leave show business. The very thought of the second thought made him feel what Adam must have felt when God chucked him the hell out of Eden. Milt would then imagine Adam's Eve wearing nothing but a fig leaf—a thought so exciting his prostate would burn like a cheap doll in a house fire.

For Milt Wagonman, show business had never been a job; it was a sacred kingdom into which he had somehow been allowed entrance. A magic fairyland where, even if not a single one of his dreams came true, he would at least be allowed to dream. What dreams could he have hoped for if he had become a nine-fingered butcher like his father? The dream of putting panties on veal chops? That's a dream? "No," he told himself, "thank you very muchly!"

And who, he asked himself, was the man who, for years, had helped him try and fulfill his deepest, permanently unfulfilled dream? None other than Marty (The X Is Silent!) Sloyxne, that's who! But how could a Milt ever make a Gwen understand the debt of gratitude, not to mention the awe, which a Milt felt toward a Marty? A shy, soft-spoken nebbish of a Milt like him? A shlub of a Milt who'd been born with none of Marty's joie de vivre? What possible chance could a Wagonman ever hope to have in the chew 'em up spit 'em out don't forget your Members Only jacket get the hell out of my office I didn't laugh once at your material don't let the door hit you in the ass as you leave big, wide, wonderful world of entertainment without a Sloyxne by his side?

Flaws? Of course Marty Sloyxne had flaws! Milt knew that! Wasn't Marty the man who had eaten couscous with his feet in a Lebanese restaurant after a waiter accused him of stealing a crate of industrial soap from the men's room storage closet? But Milt had seen other things. Great things. Milt's thoughts raced back to the time he had been so nervous at a pitch meeting for *Your Turn in the Barrel* that he had actually thrown up on the producer's half-loafers. And a particularly disgusting puke it had been, too. The terrible moment occurred at a meeting during Pesach, after Milt had eaten so much hamentashen that he'd involuntarily emitted staccato bursts of gas every time his right foot hit the pavement on his and Marty's walk from Guest Parking to the producer's office, where his puking had been as involuntary as his flatulence. Where a lot of partners would scream and shout and apologize and scold their soiled partner, Marty merely stood up, walked over to where the helpless producer sat, removed both of the man's puke-covered shoes, walked them over to a window, threw them out, turned around, told the producer to "write down your size, we'll buy you a new pair and bring 'em over to your house six o'clock tomorrow morning," and continued to pitch *Your Turn in the Barrel*.

"Every week," Marty said, soldiering on, "a different celebrity gets in a cheese barrel, see, and panelists like Kitty Carlisle Hart or Pinky Lee's widow or somebody like that has to guess who's inside, just by asking them questions through a hole in the barrel. And here's the beauty part, the celebrities use 'cute' voices until they get outa the barrel, so's nobody can tell it's them."

Milt had never been prouder of his partner than right then . . . and they might even have sold the show had Milt not thrown up a second time on the head of the producer's ten-year-old son, who had just rushed in, with his beautiful mother on his heels, to show his producer dad his new Little League uniform. You just don't get those Kodak moments outside the Business, thought Milt, but how could his wife—a woman for whom bliss was a coupon for fifty cents off on a Sara Lee Bundt cake—ever share the buzz he got from his craft where anyone with the guts, and maybe the foolishness, to try and make it gets to experience the soaring delusion that anything and everything is possible? The simple answer is Gwen could not, and so Milt had stopped trying to explain. He even stopped telling her the "vomit on the Little Leaguer" story and wrote off all the hostility she felt toward Marty now as emotional fallout from the sudden, and tragic, death of her 109-year-old mother. After all, Gwen was the first one to reach the mean old bag only moments after her head was folded into the accordion doors of the Ventura to Glendale bus. So of course Milt's wife was going to go off the deep end, what with her having been orphaned, as she was, at the age of sixty-eight.

Milt had to blame the tragedy of his mother-in-law's death for the trouble in his marriage, for if he really thought Gwen might force him to leave comedy—or, worse, never see Marty again—God knows what he might do. Although he certainly wouldn't kill himself. Milt loved eating fresh fruit, and watching *The Rockford Files*, and peeing outside at night up against the tree stump abutting the sound absorption wall next to the 101 Freeway way too much for that. But he could also never leave Gwen, so Milt was stuck between a rock and a hand brake as, even now, in his silent thoughts, he made a "funny" vis-à-vis his predicament to himself.

Meanwhile, Marty was going through his own brand of hell. For two nights in a row, since receiving the news, via telephone, that Milt was going to take a "breather" from the partnership, Marty had been desperate. Every night thereafter he slept on the Wagonman roof, waking before dawn and treating himself to a drive-in breakfast of Milt's favorite morning food—egg whites and prunes and prune juice and toast and the key to the men's room—before then ordering a second breakfast of his own favorite food—a three-egg Denver omelet plus two rashers of bacon plus mashed potatoes plus English muffins buttered on both sides—which Marty then followed up with a third breakfast of what he thought Gwen might enjoy for breakfast—a side of plain low-fat yogurt, a side of fruit, and a glass of apple juice, but nothing filled the void. Day after day, with nothing to do but brood and make phony phone calls to tobacconists—"If you have Prince Albert in a can, you better get him the hell out before he suffocates!"—Marty filled the endless evenings, before it was his time to climb onto Milt and Gwen's roof, by trolling for prostitutes under five feet in height. As if seeking some kind of weird penance for the *Shark Rider* incident, and what might turn out to be the permanent loss of his partner, Marty decided to deny himself the company of any woman of normal size. Unable to find a midget whore, he hired a six-foot, one-inch woman who charged him "to crouch over." But all Marty wanted to do was talk. He told her about his partner, Milt—about how much he loved him and how much he missed him—and when he was finished the prostitute had stolen his wallet. And, truth be told, there was the time, within a month of Milt dumping Marty, when Marty came up with the idea—just to show Milt that Milt wasn't the only "unfunny nobody" Marty could turn into a comedy writer—of teaming up with someone else just for the spite of it.

Marvin "Jocko" Benjamitz was a forty-eight-year-old idiot who spent his days outside the Farmers Market holding a blank autograph book. He idolized Milt and Marty and what he called their "big normal boy success." Back during the good times Marty would always point at Jocko and make fun of all the piss stains on his pants, but now things had changed. Marty was hurt, and he wanted to hurt back.

"Milt!" he shouted, as he and Jocko pretended to have just run into Milt and Gwen outside Milt's internist's office. "I'd like you to meet my new partner. I believe you know Mr. Benjamitz, Milt, but I don't think Gwen has ever had the pleasure!"

For a moment, Milt's astonishment superseded the pain that had been coursing through him since the moment, five minutes earlier, when his doctor had gone finger-trawling up his anus for prostate lobster.

"So," Marty said, as if finding a new partner after forty-five years with Milt was the most humdrum thing in the universe, "Jocko, here, and I will be pitching a new show to Marlo Thomas's company in ten minutes." Milt knew it couldn't possibly be true . . . not only did Jocko Benjamitz not know the first thing about comedy structure, he also wore a Mickey Mouse hat to synagogue.

"Walk on, Milton!" Gwen commanded her husband, all too aware of the game Marty was playing. Marty commanded Jocko to tell Milt the great new pilot idea they had just come up with, but Jocko wandered away when a Mr. Softee truck pulled up to the curb.

The pain of seeing Marty with another writer—even if it was Jocko Benjamitz—was enough to make Milt agree to seek counseling with Gwen. That Marty would parade another partner in front of him like that—even if the guy wasn't really a partner—well, it was beyond betrayal, and no less painful for the fact that Jocko was an imbecile who thought Gene Rayburn was the president of the United States.

Pearl Kubler-Roth had trained under the legendary Viennese psychiatrist Gunnar Gable Gunther, father of the Mirroring movement of the 1920s. The Mirroring cure involved the patient talking only to a hand mirror during analysis while consistently maintaining a facial expression of complete surprise at finding his or her own self in the reflection. Gwen had a tough time with the technique at first but came to see its value after having a breakthrough shortly after her mother's death. Although the breakthrough had excited her, she couldn't remember what it had been by the time she got to Ralph's and found that the price of Van Camp's pork and beans had been discounted to 63 cents a can.

Milt agreed to go to his wife's lady therapist, but he refused to talk into a mirror during the therapeutic process. "I'll talk into my Writers Guild card—it's shiny as heck—but that's as far as I'll go." And since the guild was paying for 80 percent of the treatment, Dr. Kubler-Roth reluctantly agreed to look the couple in the face.

Milt hadn't been in a psychiatrist's office since his army days when, after wetting his bunk in Okinawa, the company head shrinker had begun the process of trying to cure him by giving him a Rorschach test. As the shrink held up a series of flash cards emblazoned with different ink spots, Milt was supposed to say the first thing that came to his mind, but the only thing Milt saw, on eleven of the twelve cards, was Marty Sloyxne. When the shrink held up the twelfth card he asked, "Is this Marty Sloyxne too?"

"No," said Milt. "It's Ivory Deek Watson!"

"Who's that?" asked the shrink.

"One of the Ink Spots," said Milt. "Y'know . . . the singing group. Marty Sloyxne recently played one of their records for me."

Milt had just met Marty around then, and his comedy crush was in full blush. He stopped wetting his regulation army cot soon after that, but not because of any brilliant insights the army doc had offered. No, sir, what did the trick—what had finally dried up the old spigot after more than twenty embarrassing years—was Marty asking Milt to write sketches with him for "Red, White, and Jew," the USO show that Martha Raye had derived so much pleasure from.

Sitting now all these years later in couples therapy with his wife, all Milt could think of was Marty. Where was he? What was he doing? Was he okay? Did he remember to shave inside his ears?

"Milton! Milton!" Gwen whispered, sharply, tapping his hands with what Milt felt was an unnecessary harshness when Dr. Kubler-Roth looked momentarily away. Milt returned to the present and followed Gwen's worried eye to the crotch of his khaki slacks, where a small but noticeable wet spot had just appeared. Gwen laid her sweater over her husband's stain before returning her full attention to the good doctor.

"Mrs. Wagonman tells me your daughter hasn't spoken to either of you for thirty-five years?" said Dr. Kubler-Roth.

Milt, who was thrown, took a moment to find the perfect response.

"She ran off to join the lesbians."

"The lesbians are a lifestyle, Milton! They're not the circus!" Gwen whisper-shouted.

"What was the question again?" asked Milt.

Without any judgment in her tone the doctor said, "Your daughter doesn't speak to you. I think we should explore the whys of that."

"The entire whys?"

"That's what you do in therapy, honey," said Gwen, "you talk about all the whys . . . you share your innermost . . . things."

"Oh," said Milt, who hadn't really ever looked at psychotherapy from that standpoint. "What other things of a personal nature did you tell her, Gwendolyn?"

"I'm sitting right here, Mr. Wagonman. You can ask me yourself," said a friendly-sounding, yet firm-sounding, yet professional-sounding Dr. Kubler-Roth.

"I . . . uhhh . . . well . . . ," said Milt.

"I told her that you were a bedwetter in the army," said Gwen, who'd grown tired of waiting for Milt to say something and seemed, to Milt, to sound like she was proud that she had gotten comfortable enough to reveal something so intensely embarrassing about him to a stranger.

"You told her *that?* I don't believe you, Gwen!"

Gwen replied that Milt needed to drop his defenses if they were going to have any chance of getting their marriage back on an even footing. Then she lifted her sweater off Milt's lap so the doctor could see the pee stain on his slacks.

"That stain is old!" Milt said, defensively. "A guy standing next to me at a urinal splattered off the Formica two weeks ago!"

Dr. Kubler-Roth rephrased the question. "Why hasn't Randi spoken to you?"

The answer to this, and to decades of other heartbreaking questions, could be summed up in two words: Marty Sloyxne. But Milt's mouth could not form those two words. As Gwen's therapist kept her gaze leveled on him Milt started to melt. There was something in the good doctor's eyes—call it compassion, call it "you'd better hurry up and say something because you're paying for this," call it what you will—but whatever it was it made Milt want to share, to talk about the little girl he had loved so much and may have lost forever.

"Truth is, doc," he said, "Randi hasn't spoken to us in thirty-eight years. We say it's been only thirty-five 'cause it doesn't hurt as much." Milt swallowed hard and then forced himself to go on. "Sometimes I wish I had never heard of Wiki-Wachee Springs. Randi was a teen then, and she actually had a date with a boy . . . her first, maybe her last, I don't know . . . a nice boy, anyway, we were down in Florida . . . me and my partner, Marty—"

Gwen glared at him.

"—I mean, me and my ex-partner, Marty—maybe—went down to Miami on spec hoping to get work with Jackie Gleason, who'd just moved his show there. Gleason looked at our sketches but it didn't come to anything. Marty thinks the Great One didn't hire us because Jackie's shorty robe opened up during the meeting and we saw his little mushroom cap. Marty said 'that fat Irishman would never hire a writer who had seen his jiminy cricket,' but I think he was intimidated by the material. Marty had just started psychoanalysis himself, coincidentally, and all our sketches suddenly had to contain dreams Marty was having. In one, Jackie would have played Marty's mother, who had the body of a goat, and she was panning for gold in the Yukon. Another sketch envisioned Gleason portraying Czar Nicholas of Russia and—"

"Get to the point, honey," said Gwen.

"Sure," said Milt. "So Jackie passed, and we decided, Gwen and me, to take Randi up to Wiki-Wachee Springs for one of those glass-bottom boat rides. Marty came with us and slept in our room. He was sleepwalking a lot then and used to chase garbage trucks like a dog . . . it was the scariest doggoned thing. He caught one, once, and the driver nearly had a heart attack. Marty was clinging to the hood ornament in his underpants. Anyhoo, Randi had met this boy at the motel and invited him along, which was great for us because we had been real worried about Randi. She was always in my closet trying on my clothes and cutting out pictures of women in bras and hiding the pictures under her bed . . . and these were different times so we were worried she was going to be a lesbian. Now parents are worried if your kid *isn't* a lesbian . . ." Milt waited for the doctor to laugh but she just nodded for him to continue.

"Okay, so we're all in the glass-bottom boat and Randi is excited. We'd never seen her this happy when, all of a sudden, Marty lets himself over the side of the boat into the water. We didn't see him do it but we're looking at the ocean floor, and up through the glass comes this huge white monstery-looking thing. I thought it was a manatee, but it was actually Marty's ass. He had gone over the side and dropped his pants and floated his ass up to the glass like the little ASK AGAIN LATER sign in one of those Magic 8 balls. He pressed his ass right up to the glass, right there in front of my daughter and her date, who started screaming. Well, that was it. Our kid never spoke to her mother or me—or, of course, Marty—again. And she subsequently went to court to have her middle name—Sloyxne, which is the last name of her godfather, whose first name is Marty—expunged from all California state records. That hurts, y'know . . ."

The only audible sounds, during the long, long silence that followed Milt's monologue, were those of Gwen blowing her nose and Dr. Kubler-Roth removing the tinfoil from one of her imported lozenges. Finally, the doctor took off her glasses, rubbed her eyes, and crossed to the window. She stared down at the Sportsman's Lodge parking lot for a long time before turning back to the Wagonmans and saying, "There are three people in your marriage."

"Not anymore," said Milt. "My mother-in-law's head was recently trapped in a folding door."

"She's talking about Marty, Milt!" shouted Gwen.

"Jeez, Gwen, you're always ragging on Marty. She's always ragging on Marty, doctor," said Milt, who shrugged as if "ragging on Marty" was a completely irrational thing to do. "I mean, what did Marty ever do to us besides write some of the best buttons and scene blows in television history!"

Dr. Kubler-Roth asked what a "scene blow" and a "button" were and Gwen filled her in.

"The big joke," she said, "that gets you from one scene to the next."

"Which reminds me," said Dr. Kubler-Roth, not trying to hide the fact that she was looking at the clock on the wall behind Milt and Gwen, "that it's time for our scene blow."

"Good segue!" said Milt. "Marty, who is king of the segue, would have appreciated it."

"My God," said Gwen. "Can you go five minutes without bringing Marty into whatever it is that we talk about? I want this to be our therapy! I don't want him here with us! Can you understand that?"

Gwen broke down in sobs.

"Jeez, Gwennie," said Milt, jumping up and running to her side.

"This might be a good time," said Dr. Kubler-Roth, "to ask you both a final question."

Milt told the doctor he knew what she was going to ask and reassured her that he would "urinate completely" before the next session.

"That has nothing to do with what I want to ask you, Mr. Wagonman," said Dr. Kubler-Roth, "but I appreciate the consideration. What I do want to ask you, though, is whether or not you'd consider inviting Marty Sloyxne to your next session?"

"What?" gasped Gwen through her tears. "How could you ask that? Don't you see what that man does to me even when he's not here?"

"I think it would be helpful," said the doctor.

"I have no degree in psychology but I see the worth in it," said Milt, very excited by the idea.

"I think I would rather have my eyelids removed and be forced to look at the sun," Gwen replied.

"I think the two of you should think about it." With that, Dr. Kubler-Roth turned, walked back to the window, and looked down across Ventura Boulevard.

As Gwen headed for the door Milt hesitated, looked at Dr. Kubler-Roth, and said, "Could you tell me if the Sportsman's Lodge is advertising the Eight-ninety-nine Prime Rib Night on Thursday? It's usually up there on the marquee in the parking lot, but I was so nervous driving in I forgot to look." The doctor just stared at him.

"You know what, doc?" Milt told her. "You've already done so much for us I'll just check when I get downstairs."

That night over dinner Milt tried to contain his excitement. Having Marty join Gwen and him for couple's therapy would be the first break he'd gotten since his partner had fucked up their careers. But he had to play it cool. If Gwen felt that all he cared about was seeing Marty again, and not "working through their issues and stuff," she might not agree to let the Creature that Haunted Our Marriage attend. Knowing that Gwen was curled up on their bed like a depressed fetus, Milt tiptoed down the hallway to their bedroom, stuck his head in, and said to the small hillock under the covers that was Gwen, "I just want you to know that I want what you want, hon," he said. "If you don't want Marty to come to the session, that's fine with me. If you think he'll be a detriment in the forward progress of our life together as a couple, I'm right there with you, 'cause I don't want any part of anyone that will get in direct conflict with our bliss. But if, on the other hand, you feel that his presence might help us solidify our bliss with each other the way the bond of one infantryman is solidified with another in the presence of a common enemy, well, I'll support you in that. Otherwise, I don't care if I ever see the guy again. And I think you know me well enough to know that I mean that! May the god of the Israelites strike me dead if I don't!"

Milt didn't realize that Gwen, who peeked out through the bed covers as Milt left the room, could see in the dresser mirror that he had the fingers of both hands crossed behind his back, which saddened her but also made her more determined than ever to save her relationship with the deeply troubled man she loved.

An hour later, Gwen tiptoed out to the living room, where Milt was pretending to be asleep on the couch. She leaned down, kissed him gently on his forehead, and whispered, "If you want him there, baby, go ahead and ask him."

Milt, pretending that he'd been lulled from a deep unconsciousness, opened his eyes and said, "You sure, dollface?"

"Yes."

"Lemme think about it," he said.

As soon as Gwen had left the room Milt stood up, did a three-second jig in place, walked to the kitchen, opened the door, and hollered the invitation out to Marty, who had been standing under their oak tree for the past five hours with his own fingers crossed.

Marty, who was thrilled to have been asked to be part of the Wagonmans' life again, rented a tuxedo for the therapy session, just to show his gratitude and the seriousness with which he planned to take everything that might happen during his and Milt and Gwen's "special hour together." Unfortunately, he'd rented the tux during high school prom season, which meant that the only one he could find still on the racks was a Smokey Robinson and the Miracles powder blue number with long tails and a sequined cummerbund that glowed in the dark.

When the following Tuesday finally rolled around, Dr. Kubler-Roth could see that the man in "the odd blue costume" was trying very hard, during the first few minutes of their session, to look up her dress. When Milt caught Marty's eye long enough to warn him off, Marty averted his eyes and brought to his face, as if by express train, the most sincere expression he could fake.

Dr. Kubler-Roth started off by asking Marty if he had any children. Sloyxne responded, like a proud papa, that he had one son named Raymond, who was currently living in a mental institution.

"You sound somewhat proud of that fact, Mr. Sloyxne," said the doctor.

"Oh, I am!" Marty said. "It's one of the best hospitals in the country, doc. As a matter of fact, it's considered the Ivy League of insane asylums." And then Marty changed tact, telling the doctor that although he appreciated her interest she clearly hadn't invited him there to talk about himself, but rather to help Gwen "rise above her jealousy so's Milt and me can get back to doin' what we do best—not as in 'what we do better than anybody else' but as in 'what we do better than anything else we do'—which is writing comedy."

Before Gwen, who had turned crimson with fury, could respond, Milt jumped in with, "Martin, don't you dare blame Gwen for any of this! You know full well who's responsible for our temporary setback, of both the financial and the emotional variety, in the areas of our . . . human endeavors vis-à-vis the entertainment business!"

Marty thought for a second, nodded his agreement, and then spewed a venomous rant on how everything had been coming up roses for Wagonman and Sloyxne before Leopold and Sand came into their lives—how much Gwen had always respected Marty before that and how "those two young *All About Eve* stab-us-in-the-back little pricks came into the little jewel box of a life we noble and happy three had established for ourselves before those two young pretenders to our throne showed up and took a royal crap all over the very throne of which I speak!"

Dr. Kubler-Roth asked Marty to take a breath and tell her something about himself.

"Like what?"

"Like, are you currently married?"

"No."

"Have you ever been?"

"Sure! D'ya think the son I told you about is a bastard or somethin'?"

"Not at all. People do have children without ever getting—"

"Nine," said Marty.

"I beg your pardon?"

"Nine," he repeated.

"Why are you saying 'no' in German?"

"I ain't! I didn't say *nein*. I said nine, like the number. Which is the number of times I been married!"

"You've been married nine times?" asked Dr. Kubler-Roth, whose voice cracked on "times."

"With all due respect, doc," said Marty, "I can't see what the number of bad marriages one guy's been in could possibly have to do with the bad marriage another guy is currently in, and—"

"How dare you!" shouted Gwen.

"What!" shouted Marty.

"How dare he call my marriage to Milt a bad one!" shouted Gwen at Dr. Kubler-Roth.

"Tell him," said the doctor.

"How dare you call our marriage a bad one!" shouted Gwen at Marty.

"You don't have to shout it at me!" shouted Marty, who then pointed at the doctor and shouted, "I heard it when you shouted it at her!"

"Okay," said the doctor. "No more shouting. How about you talk about yourself without mentioning or alluding to the Wagonmans? Could you do that?"

"I can do anything, doc," said Marty. "Except the Saturday *New York Times* crossword puzzle. Friday? Yes, about three-tenths of it. But the Saturday one is murder!"

"Let's talk about your marriages, Mr. Sloyxne," said Dr. Kubler-Roth.

"What about 'em?"

"You tell me."

"Okay. Well, I never hit any of my wives and I'm proud of that. Some of my exes speak to me and some choose not to, for various reasons, even though there's only one real reason for it, which is that their childhoods weren't very good, but they can't admit it."

"Were you faithful to them?" asked Dr. Kubler-Roth, which caused Milt to send a high falsetto laugh bouncing off the walls of the office.

"Shut up!" shouted Marty.

"No shouting," said the doctor.

"But he laughed at my life!" shouted Marty. "The motherfucker hurt my motherfuckin' feelings!"

"Tell him. Without shouting."

"How 'bout without using the filthy language?" asked Gwen, but it was too late.

"You hurt my motherfuckin' feelings, motherfucker," said Marty to Milt.

"Still with the filthy mouth," said Gwen.

"I'm sorry, Martin," said Milt.

"Don't apologize to him!" shouted Gwen.

"No shouting!" shouted Marty.

"May we continue, please?" asked the doctor, in a voice trained not to get angry.

"Sorry," said Gwen and Milt.

"Mr. Sloyxne?" said the doctor. "Please continue."

"I cheated during six of my honeymoons," said Marty. "Which is not a bad average for a guy married as many times as I was. None of the women ever caught me cheating on them, which, again, I'm proud of and which is a fact, I think, that shows the kind of reverence I held for the sacramental sanctity of marriage." Marty wanted to stop talking after that but he thought of a good button for the speech. "One more thing, doc, if you'll permit me?"

"Of course," said Dr. Kubler-Roth.

"Every single time I cheated on one of my wives—and it happened pretty much every week—I would stop making love to her for at least a month, just to make sure they wouldn't catch anything. 'Cause I'll tell you something, Dr. Ruth—"

"It's Dr. Kubler-*Roth*."

"—some of the women I threw a batch into in them days—excuse my French—had infections that could stop a train!"

"I think I'm getting sick," muttered Gwen.

"How would you sum up the way you feel about marriage, Mr. Sloyxne?" asked the doctor.

"How would I sum it up?" said Marty. "I guess I'd just say that when it comes to marriage, I just didn't—as I did in my career—get the right cards."

Dr. Kubler-Roth, who was nothing if not professional, was able to keep almost 20 percent of the disgust she felt off her face as she asked Gwen to respond to what Marty had just shared. Gwen, when she found her voice, said only that she was glad the doctor could see for herself the "kind of filthy lunatic my husband looks up to."

Marty, touched by the remark, whispered to Milt that he looked up to him as well, and then he said to Gwen, "Y'know, Gwen, they called Rasputin a lunatic, too, and he did pretty darned good for himself!" Pleased with himself, Marty took a Reuben sandwich out of his pants pocket, offered half of it around, and commandeered what was left of the session. "Doc, with all due respect, blah, blah, blah, this is getting us nowhere. Look, if it means anything to anybody, at this late date, I'll come out and say the words I know everybody's waiting for a Marty Sloyxne to say. I'm not a proud man but I am a truth teller, and if I have any faults, or have maybe made a mistake or two in my life, I own up to 'em because that's what a truth teller does!" Marty took a big bite of his sandwich, washed it down with a gulp of Dr. Kubler-Roth's Darjeeling iced tea, and stood and faced the Wagonmans. "Milt,

Gwen, I'd like to say something now which I hope you accept in the spirit for which it's intended."

Gwen, thinking naively that an apology was on the way, did what a Gwen Wagonman does, she was gracious. "Go ahead, Martin," she said. A grateful Milt took his wife's hands in his own.

"And before I say what needs to be said," Marty said, enjoying the limelight, "I'd like to thank you, Dr. Ruth, for your spirit and guidance on our journey here today . . ."

"You're welcome, Mr. Sloyxne," said the doctor. "But it's Dr. Kubler-*Roth*."

"Whatever," Marty said and then turned once more toward Gwen and Milt, got on one knee, and spoke from his heart.

"Guys," he said. "Coming closer than close to almost losing you two beautiful people, I need for you to know that—well—I now believe, once again, in the existence of sharks."

"That's it!" shouted Gwen, who shot to her feet and grabbed for her coat, turning back only to shout at Milt, "Your rotten partner has ruined couples therapy for me forever!"

Ignoring a plea from Dr. Kubler-Roth to return to the couch, Gwen swung the door wide, told Milt he had twenty-four hours to decide between her and Marty, and left the office.

"Where's she running?" Marty asked Milt, going, even now, for the laugh. "I don't have to return the tux until six!"

Had Milt not felt a chill that ran the length and breadth of his spine at that moment, he might have been able to say something, or at least go after his wife.

"What the hell did I say, anyway?" asked Marty of Dr. Kubler-Roth. "I thought we were supposed to be honest in this room!"

Later, downstairs in the Sportsman's Lodge parking lot, Milt was not only inconsolable but without a ride. Marty offered Milt that ride but Milt, feeling it would be disloyal to his wife, politely refused.

"Oh, my car's not good enough for you now, Mr. Couples Therapy?" said Marty. "Well, let me tell you something, Mr. My Shit Don't Stink. Your shit stinks fine, just fine! Your shit stinks great, Milty!" Try as he might, Milt couldn't help but laugh at that one, and then laughed harder as Marty, his partner, sent a giant "B-waaaaaaa!" out into the late afternoon air.

Marty patted Milt on the shoulder and sat down on the curb next to him, careful to take his tuxedo jacket off, folding it first. A Plymouth sped by, splashing dirty puddle water all over them but they didn't mind.

"Look, pally," said Marty, not unaware that Milt had always loved it when he called him "pally." "I been thinkin', during the last week or so, about everything we been through—all the ridiculous shit . . . and I suddenly realize that you and me, we took the wrong fork in the road, way back when. Two golden comedy minds like ours never shoulda been wasted in television, man! Guys as savvy and sophisticated—not to mention as fuckin' funny—as us? We shoulda been writin' for movies all along, partner! Movies, Mr. Schmuck Master General, movies! Whaddya say, brother? You with me or not? You gonna join your Marty in the transformation of Wagonman and Sloyxne from shit-hook sitcom bottom feeders to powerful major fuckin' domos in the elite screenwriting fraternity? You got seventy-two hours to gimme a yes or no, brother, and that's, well, I can't do the math but it's more hours than your own wife gave you . . . think about that, your own *wife*!"

By the time his bus finally came and he caught up to his wife, Milt found Gwen still dazed and walking the aisles of the very same dollar store where, forty-six years earlier, she had proposed marriage to her even then pathetically shy husband. When she came face to face with Milt across from the oven mitt bin, she looked in his apologetic eyes and said, in a bare whisper, "Well, what's your decision?"

Milt, summoning all the explaining talent he had honed in story meetings, laid out all the "severe psychological dilemma feelings" Marty had just put on him by saying they should write movies.

"The man may be crazy," he said, "but what he says about him and me taking the wrong fork in the road, way back when, makes a lot of sense. You know how I've always felt about movies, Gwennie. I know you know because you and I, when we first met, we shared the same passion for 'em. Remember that second week we knew each other, back in '54, when we saw twelve of 'em over the course of five days? I can rattle off their names, even now: *On the Waterfront, La Strada, 20,000 Leagues Under the Sea . . .*"

Gwen, who didn't remember seeing any of those movies, sighed and said, "Look, I can't win here, Milt! Nothing I say or do will keep you from Marty and the further degradation of our lives . . ."

"So I have your blessing then?" Milt couldn't believe his ears.

Then Gwen reminded Milt of why he loves her so much. "Go off, my crazy husband, and write your crazy movie with your crazy partner," she told him.

"Really? You mean it? You won't be mad at me?"

"Listen to me, and listen well," said she. "I love you more than anything else in the world, more even than a good life. So go write your cinema. But before you do I have just one request."

"Anything, my darling!"

"Make your nice love to me."

"Here in the dollar store?"

"No. Home."

Milt & Marty

Once back home, Milt did what Gwen had asked him to do, preparing himself, during foreplay, as he always did and always will, for the seemingly incongruous yet inevitable moment, which for some reason has always occurred, and will seemingly always occur, during the act of the Wagonmans' lovemaking, when the otherwise delicate, refined, and occasionally ethereal Gwen says, in Yiddish mind you, as she always had during their act of love and evidently always will, "Split me in half, Daddy Longlegs, with your big blue Seabiscuit cock!"

CRUCIFIED ON THE HOLLYWOOD SIGN

||||||||||||||||||||||||||

The first thing Marty said to Milt when Milt returned to the partnership fourteen minutes after pleasuring his wife was, "I knew you wouldn't pussy out on me." The second and most important thing Marty said was that he'd written a one-page story outline for a movie "kinda like *The Robe* . . . a biblical tale, the likes of which my instinct tells me is gonna be the next hot thing in this go-go culture of ours."

"A biblical idea?" Milt thought it was genius. "But tell me, Martin, how did the idea come to you?" Marty said the idea fell into his mind after he, for some reason, had a vision, back during their therapy session, of "Dr. Ruth in a bikini up on a cross on the wall behind my bed."

Milt was eager to get started. He had loved Bible stories ever since an elderly rabbi he'd known as a child scared the hell out of him with a tale of a dybbuk who "rose vertically out of the mist in the Shlee woods screaming *"Bash-a-lom-fa-la-lheem-bash-leem!"* which, he said, meant "eat all little boys!" The rabbi—who, it later turned out, was found to have dementia and was not even Jewish—had instilled a love of the old ways in Milt, making him now eager to pass the torch along on the big screen.

"Here's what we're going to do, kid"—Milt loved it when Marty called him "kid"—"you and yours truly here"—and Milt loved it even more when Marty called himself "yours truly"—"are going to pitch the picture, before it's even written, to that bright young acting talent Mr. Harry Shearer.

"Harry Shearer?" said Milt. "You mean the kid who cowrote that first Albert Brooks movie?"

"Mondo same-o!" said Marty. Marty was talking at about a hundred miles an hour now. He had glimpsed their future and wanted Milt to glimpse it too before they both got too tired and had to take a nap. "For instance, Harry's shooting a picture in Griffith Park tomorrow. I read about it in a copy of *Variety* somebody left in my gas station's crapper."

"So?" Milt asked, confused but always eager to share in anyone's enthusiasm.

"So? I'll give you a *so*, my friend!" Marty reminded Milt how the team of Wagonman and Sloyxne had befriended Shearer back in the fifties when the team acted as scabs during a writers' strike on the old Jack Benny program. Shearer, then a child actor, who would later grow up to star in such comedy classics as *This Is Spinal Tap*, had been playing a Boy Scout to Jack Benny's troop leader when Milt and Marty struck up an on-set friendship with the gifted child. Milt even offered to share his lunch with Harry after Marty stole Harry's lunch along with the kid's bus fare home. Soon, after the Benny episode wrapped, Harry went on to win the coveted role of Richard Burton as a boy in the biblical epic *The Robe*, and for some odd but completely in character reason Marty begrudged the eleven-year-old's success.

"That snot-nosed kid!" Marty ranted for days at the Brown Derby. "He could've put a word in for us on the Bible picture. We fed that ungrateful cocker lunch for crissakes!"

Milt had tried to calm his partner by reminding Marty that a middle-aged man, carrying 260 pounds on a six-three frame, had no chance of playing Richard Burton as a boy or, for that matter, Richard Burton as a man. Furious at Milt's lack of imagination, Marty fired back, "They could've built a trench for me to walk in so I'd look small! It's movie magic, you dumb heeb! They do it all the time. Look at Alan Ladd, for crying out loud." Milt thought of arguing with Marty and telling him that on the Ladd movies it was the *other* actors who walked in trenches, but then he thought better of it.

Each succeeding decade brought a whole new bunch of people to hate, and Marty had forgotten all about Harry Shearer until that afternoon when he had, for some reason, envisioned Dr. Kubler-Roth waiting for him to crucify her. A vision that not only brought back Marty's long-buried rage about Shearer's "beating me out of the Richard Burton part," but seemed to be a divine sign of just how he and Milt should go about crashing the gates of "film-writing-dom"!

On the afternoon following Marty's "*Robe* rage," as he called it, Tom and Bob had stopped off for an after-work beer at Joe Allen's on 3rd Street in order to wait for the rush hour traffic to pass and also to see how many additional people might kiss their asses now that they had a hit show on the air. Tom found his old friend Harry Shearer sitting all alone at the bar knocking back a double Stoli on the rocks. Harry seemed uncharacteristically down, but after being plied by the boys with a plate of deep-fried potato skins Harry was able to share a story with them that was, in every way but the details, all too familiar.

"I ran into a couple of guys you know today," said Harry.

"Yeah? Who?" asked Bob.

"Wagonman and Sloyxne."

Tom and Bob choked on their potato skins as Harry, who was clearly still in shock from whatever had happened to him this day, continued his story.

"I love Wagonman and Sloyxne, always have, and as you know, guys, I played Richard Burton as a boy in *The Robe* in 1953, and for some fucked-up reason, which I found out today from Marty Sloyxne, himself, Marty Sloyxne himself still had it in his insane head that after production ended on the film, way back then, I kept the robe which the Jesus character wore in the picture, when the truth was that there were many, many backup robes in the wardrobe department. I never took any of them home because I was just a naive kid who didn't think that it was my right to steal from whatever production I was in . . ."

Harry took a minute to compose himself, order another vodka, and sign an autograph for a woman whose favorite film had always been *The Robe*.

"Well, anyway, flash forward and I'm shooting a scene in an industrial film for the Encyclopedia Britannica people. And we're on location today up on Mulholland Drive near the Hollywood sign when one of the grips on the picture notices what looks to be one very old guy being crucified up on the gigantic second 'L' of the Hollywood sign by another, even older-looking guy, who seems to be wearing Roman soldier garb. So after I shoot my scene I have one of the Teamsters drive me over to the sign and, sure enough, there's Milt Wagonman who, at Marty Sloyxne's insistence, had just nailed Marty, with real four-inch nails, up onto the 'L.' Marty spots me and starts screaming that he won't come down until I agree to read a spec one-page outline he and his partner wrote about a child actor who steals Jesus' robe from a Bible picture he's acting in and how this kid actor comes to be worshipped as the Messiah by the members of the Screen Actors Guild and its sister unions. Marty has lost a lot of blood by now, so I promise to sit down on a rock with the page, which was pretty unintelligible, what with the God knows what kinds of stains all over it, but I pretend to fall in love with the project just to get Marty to come down off the sign. By now the paramedics are there and they have to attach Marty to those medical jumper cables to get his heart going. It was a helluva thing and Marty, after they stabilize him and lift him into the ambulance and everything, looks down at one of the paramedics—an Asian guy—and tells him that if he will accept Marty as his one true lord and savior, Marty will heal him of his Asian eyes so they can be round and 'normal like a white guy's eyes'! I swear to God it was a tribute to this medic's oath of office that he could find it within himself to keep Marty alive after that bullshit. Maybe that was the miracle . . ."

Stunned, all Tom and Bob could do was feel relief at never having played Richard Burton as a boy. Bob made a mental note to send Marty a basket of those little muffins in the hospital, while out in Joe Allen's parking lot they waited for the matching Lexuses they had each just paid cash for and congratulated themselves for having survived with their lives the horror known as Milt and Marty.

After pulling a groin muscle while masturbating, Marty had to stay in the hospital longer than expected. When Bob Sand's basket of "little muffins" arrived on the day Milt had come to take him home, Marty made Milt dump them into his full bedpan and toss them into an electrical closet. Milt tried to talk Marty into letting him keep the little muffins but Marty insisted that he wanted nothing from those "Leopold and Sand fuckers, and besides they got piss all over them now!" Marty told Milt that the reason "the Shearer kid" didn't bite on their movie idea was that they didn't offer the actor a completed spec script instead of the one-page beat sheet with Factor's Deli pastrami stains on it, which Shearer, that "ungrateful young shit-ass," dropped on the ground like "it was ca-ca!" But always happy to learn from any setback Marty decided to abandon biblical-type stories completely and try something more modern, which kids might "spark to" now that they "spend all day sticking marijuana in their arms and snorting patchouli oil."

"So, Martin," Milt said, wheeling Marty in a wheelchair from the hospital toward Milt's parking space in the hospital garage. "Got any ideas yet?"

"No."

"Oh," said Milt, suddenly too depressed to remember where he'd parked his car. "Would you fuckin' look at us?" shouted Marty. "Two beaten old sons of bitches who can't find their fuckin' car! We're like two spent matches afloat in the crapper of a Beverly Wilshire banquet floor men's room, Milty, waiting for the bar mitzvah boy's fat self-conscious uncle, who just snapped a prizewinning stinkfish, to flush us into the sewers of Beverly Hills."

With that, Milt told Marty that if by some miracle he was able to find his car he thought that he'd just go home and lie down for a couple of days.

"Not so fast, my friend!" Marty suddenly bounced back. The ol' wheels were turning. "Now, shut your ass, Wagonman, and let the master think."

In a rare moment of philosophical clarity Marty Sloyxne decided then and there that he and his trusty sidekick would return to the source, meaning they would study the classic, culture-altering films of the past, the ones that had "touched a billion worldwide souls at once," and write the sequel to one of them, gauging their decision on which one it would be "by watching all the originals and figuring out which one the world once hooked its heart and soul to most deeply and most deeply needs to be reunited with right now."

Wagonman and Sloyxne became fixtures at the Hollywood branch of the LA Public Library, where they worked while seated among a diverse mix: earnest LA City College students; Hollywood-area retirees; alcoholic transients and teenaged runaway druggies; a ponytailed serial killer on the lam from the Pacific Northwest who had waited in the car, back in 1959, when Perry Smith and Richard Hickock slaughtered the Clutter family in Holcomb, Kansas, but whose participation in the crime had, for some reason, gone unreported; and several respectable-looking married businessman types who hadn't yet officially come out but titillated themselves by sitting in close proximity to the legendary men's room where they liked to imagine that an easy million acts of vigorous same-sex coupling had taken place.

Milt and Marty studied the cultural dips and rises of the previous half century by watching dozens upon dozens of movies, assisted in their quest by library cinema specialist Dawn Duvall, who gave them unlimited access over the course of three months to her beloved film vault. They viewed ninety-one great movies of the past before deciding that the one that would most likely be their "express ticket to the big time" must be a sequel to *Star Wars*, which had, after all, been about the ignorance, greed, lust, self-obsession, and self-destructiveness of the human species. They decided to call their sequel *The Empire Strikes Out* and were so excited by the sudden rush of hope they both felt coursing through their veins that they decided to hole themselves up in the attic of the secluded Laurel Canyon home their new best friend, Dawn, had offered them as a sanctuary in which they would do nothing but write. "This is gonna be it for us, baby!" said Marty. "Because we are going to mix two great genres—the George Lucas-esque futuristic morality tale and the time-proven box office winner which is the fuckin' baseball movie!"

For eleven intense days, the only time either of them pulled themselves away from their matching IBM electric typewriters, which Dawn had so graciously borrowed on their behalf from the library, was to eat the delicious food Gwen would bring by Dawn's six times a day, sleep, or go to the bathroom. During those eleven days and nights, during which Milt and Marty slept a total of thirty-one hours, they didn't read newspapers, or watch TV, or listen to the radio, or even glance at the copies of *Variety* and the *Hollywood Reporter* to which Dawn, as an LA film person of sorts, felt obligated to subscribe. All they did was write. And in the early afternoon of their twelfth straight day as completely focused, totally committed seventy-one- and seventy-two-year-old novice screenwriters, respectively, they had before them on Dawn's grandmother's antique rolltop desk a 119-page beauty of a script that they knew was everything—interesting and compelling and scary and enlightening and funny and thought-provoking and breathtaking and oh-so-visual—every great film ever made had ever been. They had a hit on their hands and they knew it. They decided, before going off to their separate guest rooms to take much-deserved (separate yet synchronized) naps, to splurge and enjoy a celebratory dinner that evening at Chasen's restaurant, where they normally would have had to make a reservation two to five weeks in advance, but where Dawn had an in through her friendship with Dave Chasen's wife, Maud, who, as a Friend of the Hollywood Library, had come to know Dawn as the supreme spokeswoman for the preservation and advancement of the cultural miracle commonly known as "the Hollywood movie."

Eager to look their best for the celebration, Marty borrowed the sport jacket and slacks Dawn's deceased husband had gotten married in while Milt, of course, wore what was left of his lucky pants.

Milt and the lovely Mrs. Wagonman and Marty Sloyxne made their way to Chasen's. Raucous laughter filled the car as it approached the stoplight at the corner of Laurel Canyon and Sunset Boulevard. Moments after Milt made the right turn onto Sunset, though, all the laughter stopped and was replaced by the kind of shocked silence that can only be called cacophonous. For there on the famous Strip, looming over the boys like a death warrant, was a fading billboard trumpeting the release of a film that had broken all existing box office records when it had opened four years earlier . . . a film called *The Empire Strikes Back*, which, according to the information on the billboard, was "now breaking box office records in 1,794 theaters nationwide!"

Crushed by this latest cruel and undeserved setback, Marty decided then and there to "chuck it fuckin' all" and move to New York City and work in the legitimate theater, where he believed "an author's words still mean something and all that shit!"

"Couldn't you wait until we at least have dinner?" Milt asked.

Seventy-nine hours later Marty stepped off a train in the Big Appleton's Grand Central station and found a forty-dollar-a-night hotel room with walls so thin he could hear the guy next door change his mind. Maybe it was the city's hustle, or maybe it was its bustle, but Marty Sloyxne was already thinking like a real writer. Money and plain women suddenly meant nothing to him.

"Touching an audience of living, breathing nobodies . . . that's what it's all about!" Marty shouted aloud in Times Square in the vocal equivalent of Mary Tyler Moore tossing her ugly hat in the air. Except that was a sitcom whose producers wouldn't hire Marty and this was real life!

LONG DAY'S JOURNEY INTO NATE

||||||||||||||||||||||||||||

As for Milton Abraham Lincoln Wagonman? Well, if his wife hadn't pulled him off that train platform in Glendale he'd still be waving at the back of Marty's New York–bound Amtrak, begging his partner to "shoulder roll off the train, Martin! Shoulder roll and come home!" But there was no coming home now. Marty was doing what all the great playwrights he never bothered to read did, which was to write himself a masterpiece! And to do that one must write about what one knew. So, for the first week, Marty wrote about Milt. But strange as it sounds for someone who had spent almost fifty years elbow to elbow with the guy, Marty couldn't remember one single interesting thing about Milt. Instead, Marty decided to write about someone a little closer to home . . . but when writing about Milt's father yielded even less dramatic fodder for him, the thought struck Marty that he should write about his own father, Nathan (The X Is Silent) Sloyxne. After all, didn't someone once tell him that Eugene O'Neill had written about his father in a play called *Long Day's Journey into* . . . something? And didn't that play go on to win some kind of prize?

And so it came to be that Marty would write the story that had pent up inside him for more years than he cared to remember. The work would go through many name changes but the one that would finally stick—the title that said it all, the one Marty hoped would bring him that long-deferred respect and make him the darling of the "illiterati," as he called them—was *Long Day's Journey into Nate.* It would tell the story of "a sweet, brilliant, misunderstood jewel of a cowlicked boy" and his "gruff, mean, ignorant ape of a father."

Meanwhile, after spending two weeks trying to absorb the fact that he and Gwen were worth a grand total (including his Falcon, Gwen's '57 Chevy Biscayne, and Milt's father's Masonic ring) of $4,313.90, Milt said good-bye to the Business in order to go to work for his wealthy brother-in-law, Norjoold Hamskjold, a Swedish nudist who, in 1958, had been acquitted of murdering Milt's only sibling, his sister Harriet, and whom Milt despised. Although Milt never for a moment doubted that "Norjy Boy" (as everyone, even the judge who tried the case, called him) had killed Harriet, he was too desperate for money to refuse the job offer the man made him—especially in light of the fact that Gwen, whose fear of winding up destitute was at least as intense as Milt's, had not gotten out of bed (not even to go to the bathroom) since Wagonman and Sloyxne had become a team of the past, and that when she wasn't sobbing in a wakeful state about making history with Milt as "the only two Jews who ever had to go on welfare" she was asleep and having nightmares about it.

Norjoold Hamskjold hired Milt (at what Milt described as "a salary on the low end of the livable scale") to manage one of the seven Orange County beachfront nudist apartment complexes he owned along the Newport to Laguna Beach "naked mile." Milt and Gwen lived overlooking the pristine sand at Laguna in a one-bedroom unit at the Pink Jaybird Apartments, where they became the only two residents of the complex who remained clothed from morning to night, refusing the somewhat high-pressured efforts of their neighbors to sign up for Nude Badminton, Nude Jogging, Nude Hiking, Nude Tai-chi, and Nude Croquet classes. As worried as Milt had started to become after the *Shark Rider* tragedy about "the precarious nature of Gwen's mental stability," he was now equally relieved to be away from "the psychotic pressure cooker," as he described it, "which was the Business."

Unfortunately, his feeling of relief lasted halfway through his third day on the job, when his buck-naked next-door neighbor Jim Wagner, the wildly-less-successful older brother of actor Robert Wagner, knocked on his door, said, "Welcome to the neighborhood," asked him if he could talk to him "for less than a door-to-door dildo salesman's minute," and proceeded, almost before the cheeks of his beefy bare pink ass and undersides of his semiatrophied bare pink balls had landed on Milt's brand-new hundred percent denim La-Z-Boy recliner, to pitch him "an idea I'm reasonably certain my brother, Bob Wagner, will want to participate in after you write him a beautiful pilot script!"

"What's the idea?" asked Milt.

"That's totally up to you," said Jim.

"I beg your pardon?"

"He's shopping around for a project, and—wait, you are a TV writer like Norjy Boy said, right?"

"Well . . . "

"I mean a has-been—wait, no, that's not right—I mean you had been, right? Till recently, right?"

"Yes."

"Well, then, it looks like you and me are home free!"

"I wish it were that easy, my friend."

"It is, Milt, it is that easy, and do you wanna know why?"

"If you please."

"Because my kid brother will do anything I tell him."

"He will?"

"How do you think he wound up doing *Halls of Montezuma*, *The Happy Years*, *The Frogmen*, *Let's Make it Legal*, *What Price Glory*, *Stars and Stripes Forever*, *With a Song in My Heart*, the 1953 version of *Titanic*, *The Silver Whip*, *Beneath the Twelve-Mile Reef*, and *Prince Valiant*?"

"No kidding?"

"I care too much about this project to kid you." Not to mention: "And *Broken Lance*, *White Feather*, *Between Heaven and Hell*, *The Mountain*, *A Kiss Before Dying*, *The True Story of Jesse James*, and *Stopover Tokyo*?"

"How about *The Hunters*, *In Love and War*, *All the Fine Young Cannibals*, and *Sail a Crooked Ship*?" Milt wanted to know.

"We didn't speak to each other between 1958 and 1960," said Jim Wagner, "but we reconciled in early '61."

"That's nice for you," said Milt.

"When can I expect to have that script in my hands?"

"Give me forty-eight hours," said Milt.

"That long?"

"You can have it fast or you can have it *good*."

"I have a feeling you can do both, Milt," said Jim Wagner, who, before standing up, pinched off a squeek-fart into the La-Z-Boy, then said, "Somebody hear a mouse?" Jim thanked Milt for hearing him out and left him to the "creative process."

Milt was ashamed of himself for not having been able to tell Jim Wagner that he'd lost his fervor for the Business, not to mention his ability to concentrate on anything for more than thirty seconds at a time.

The spec script Milt sat down and wrote in spite of his ennui was called *I. Missmarty*, the title character of which was a woman named

Iris Missmarty who worked as a demure private secretary during the day and a bombastic roller derby star at night.

The role that Milt crafted for Robert Wagner was that of series host, who would appear as himself each week and introduce that night's episode. Milt handed Jim Wagner the finished script two hours and thirtynine seconds after Jim had recruited him to write it. Three days later, Milt started wondering if Robert Wagner—or even Jim, for that matter—had read it. One month after that, Milt finally conjured the nerve to approach Jim and ask him about it. He knocked on Jim's door, which was opened by a naked woman who had one of those demeanors that made her look like she could have been anywhere between fifty-five and seventy but whose breasts—which looked like two dead Airedale puppies affixed, somehow, to her chest and whose respective petrified noses rested on either side of her navel—made Milt guess she was somewhere closer to dead.

"Is Jim here?" he asked.

"Jim?" she said.

"Jim Wagner," said Milt.

"Oh, you mean that nut who says he's Robert Wagner's brother but really isn't?"

"He's not?"

"The jerk's been gone a good six weeks or so, and I got tired of waitin' on that autographed photo he promised he'd send me—quote *tomorrow* unquote—of his brother and Stefanie Powers as a show of gratitude, as he put it, for lettin' him sleep here an extra week 'cause, as he put it, the new Beverly Hills house he bought 'wasn't quite ready for a move-in.' So I asked an LA detective friend of mine if he'd check up on the cocksucker and whaddya know? It turns out that Prince Valiant never had a brother named Jim. Matter of fact, he never had a brother!"

As the manager of the complex, Milt couldn't believe that he hadn't known Jim had moved. As a comedy writer, though, he could very well believe that the guy had disappeared without saying one word about his script, or that he wasn't who he said he was. It's like I never left the Business, he thought. Milt could have absorbed that disappointment; it was not hearing from Marty that gnawed at him like one of those animals that come out at night and gnaw at things.

Back in New York City, that "defiant bitch of a town," Marty found that becoming the greatest playwright in the English language was harder than they made it look in the movies. Forced to augment his meager income of zero dollars per week, he took a job as story doctor on a dismal Broadway musical called *Countertop the Clown*. In his recently published biography, late night TV's hippest bandleader, Paul Shaffer, wisely deleted the following passage from the Canadian and Japanese editions: "When I came down to New York from Thunder Bay, Canada, I didn't have any money, so I'd get work as a rehearsal pianist for Broadway shows, or whatever . . . So my first winter there, I get hired to rehearse a new musical that this guy I'd never heard of—Marty Slone (sp?)—helped write jokes for called *Countertop the Clown*. I'm still not sure what it was about, but it had something to do with a lonely kitchen countertop that wished to become a live boy and get hired as a clown for kids' parties and civic events . . . and there were these weird characters in the show like a sponge that felt that no one could see past the holes in its face, and a box of baking soda that was always reading *The Diary of Anne Frank*. But, you know, I was so new to Broadway and 'real' show business that I never really questioned how much *Countertop the Clown* wasn't like *Hello, Dolly* or other shows I'd seen. I just accepted it all and tried to improve the musical arrangements, which wasn't that easy because Marty had written one of the songs, too, which sounded note for note like the *Perry Mason* TV program theme. Oh, and there was this Orthodox rabbi who put up all the money for the show, but only on the condition that the scenic designer use a bedsheet with a hole cut in the center of it—the same hole the rabbi used to make love to his wife Michva through—as a scrim behind the scene where Countertop the Clown—who was, by the way, a Jewish countertop—expresses his love for a sexy Gentile tin of kitchen bacteria. I left the show early on in rehearsal because, as a Jew, I was offended by the use of the sheet. The show never opened anyway. I heard Marty poured lighter fluid on the choreographer, or something, and set fire to the poor guy's dance belt."

Depressed by his monumental struggle to "find the greatness" in his play, Marty worked through the rough patches of *Long Day's Journey into Nate* by reading some of its early drafts to a blind widow, Mrs. Walter Hofnerbass, in his new role as a Read Your Un-Produced Play Aloud Volunteer at the Manhattan Braille Institute. Not only did it make Marty feel useful, but the tomato soup at the institute was always hot and full of croutons, plus Mrs. Hofnerbass just happened to be the mother-in-law of none other than Mitzi Newelpost-Whitetower, owner of the George Maharis Experimental Theatre of Hell's Kitchen.

Marty decided that he would read Mrs. Hofnerbass his now four-act play about the life-destroying relationship he'd had with his father, Nate Sloyxne, who for thirty-nine years (1917–56) made his living as a sanitation engineer—"The only kike fuckin' garbage man in the entire fuckin' history of the New fuckin' York City Sanitation fuckin' Department!" as Marty liked to boast—in the hope that her daughter-in-law would bring her heartless ass down to visit, listen to his play, and help Marty get his great work produced! Sadly for Mrs. H., and sadder even for Marty, the one night Mitzi did show up Marty was at a porno house on 42nd Street watching *Clitty Clitty Bang Bang*.

Sunrise found Marty crafting his play in the tiny sublet he'd found at 161 West Fourth Street. Directly across the hall lived Arthur Gelb, a recently retired eighty-four-year-old math teacher who'd spent the past forty-six years working at the Dalton School and was struggling with the realization that his life would most likely not, at its end, include the knowledge of what it had been like to achieve fame and fortune as a thespian. Gelb had heard Marty reciting dialogue from *Nate* at the top of his lungs every night and was sufficiently enthusiastic about it to pass it along to Fiona Ulyssa Coelho-Kennedy, a sixty-seven-year-old performance artist known to her legion of fans as F.U.C.K., who was running the midnight Teddy Gottlieb show—Teddy, of course, being the transcendent soul known professionally as Brother Theodore—at the Circle in the Square Theater in Greenwich Village and who, according to legend, had until six months before made her home on a houseboat in the Mekong Delta, where she'd taught theater improv to wounded Vietcong. Any play having anything to do with a man hating his father appealed to F.U.C.K., and she decided, after one reading of the still unfinished manuscript, to throw all of the Circle's resources behind a full-blown production.

Marty, whose initial feeling about F.U.C.K. was that she was "a pompous pain-in-the-ass liberal intellectual traitor to America who thinks she's the most interesting living organism to come along since the ocean," was beside himself—his favorite position—after a wine-soaked uptown dinner he had with her during which she revealed to him that she hadn't spent her last six months in Vietnam at all. "I was at Sing Sing," she told him, "doing three-to-five on a bunco rap."

"Holy shit!" he shouted at Times Square again. "This is just like how it happens in the movies!" Overjoyed, and immobilized with fright at his good fortune, Marty ran to the nearest pay phone. "Milt, get your flat, white, hairless heeb ass to New York pronto!"

"Martin, is that you?" Milt couldn't believe his ears; it was the collect call he dared not dream would ever come.

"Listen, you idiot," Marty barked as he stretched the phone out of the booth and held it toward the heavens. "Listen to the sweet symphony of the city! This is where you fuckin' belong, you fuck! I need you, you talented pile of shit!"

It didn't take Milt two minutes after Marty sent up that glorious SOS for him to pick a pointless fight with his dear lady wife and hop the first discount flight to New York.

Milt had to have himself thrown out of the house. For however much like money in the bank it sounded to him, to Gwen Marty's sure-fire hit show would mean nothing. Especially after he had just sunk his time and his heart into a script for an ex-neighbor who was not then, and most likely never would be, Robert Wagner's brother. So Milt did the unthinkable; he lied to the woman who had meant the stars and the moon to him for over forty-five years and said the one thing he knew would make her furious enough not to cry if he left, which was, "Gwen . . . your meat loaf just lays there!"

Hellos were barely exchanged before Milt and Marty settled down to work. The task of fixing a second, third, and fourth act and epilogue of *Long Day's Journey into Nate* was a rough row to hoe, but hoe they did, harnessed once again to each other dramaturgically and loving every mother f'ing minute of it.

The play was so close to Marty, and so full of themes he had yet to work through, that Milt was afraid, at first, to voice an opinion. But Marty knew he was too close to the material and was ready for the man who knew him best to "be cruel, my partner! Be cruel with my words!" which enabled Milt to be honest—brutally honest—about what he read.

"I love every word of it, Martin! Touch one word of it and I'll kill you!" Milt said, after which he was quickly embraced.

"Godammit, I knew it was good!" Marty said, pulling off his pants and snapping Milt in the eye with them. His writing work done, Milt's job became keeping Marty calm enough to get through opening night.

And what a night it was. The audience was packed to the rafters with twenty-six people who knew a thing or two about the theater and had an "I dare you to dazzle me" chip on their shoulders. A chip that first-time playwright Martin Sloyxne was only too happy to knock off.

At eight o'clock on a sultry June night in the year of our Lord 1989, the curtain rose for the very first time on *Long Day's Journey into Nate*. A hush fell upon the audience and the 238-minute play began.

LONG DAY'S JOURNEY INTO NATE*

A Play in Four Acts
by Martin Sloyxne

ACT ONE

Ten-year-old MARTY SLOYXNE *stands lit by a lone spotlight on a bare stage and screams, over and over again, for fifty-four minutes, one emotionally charged word.*

MARTY: Dad!

ACT TWO

Twenty-two-year-old Marty Sloyxne sits in a chair next to a hospital bed where his father, seventy-seven-year-old NATE SLOYXNE, *lies in a coma. For one hour and thirty-nine minutes Marty whimpers, over and over again, one emotionally charged question.*

MARTY: Dad?

ACT THREE

Sixty-one-year-old Marty Sloyxne crouches with a shovel next to the grave of his father, Nate, whose gravestone reads DEATH SUCKS BUT LIFE WAS WORSE, *and, for fifty-nine minutes, digs and digs and digs, deeper and deeper and deeper, into the earth toward his father's coffin. At the end of minute 31, Marty stops and exhales.*

* The play is reproduced in full with the cooperation of the Samuel French Company.

Milt & Marty

MARTY: Fuck you, Dad.

Marty pauses, then walks offstage, throwing the shovel into the newly dug hole as he exits.

ACT FOUR

Seventy-three-year-old Marty Sloyxne stands in a room at an unknown state mental institution and listens as his son, the severely mentally ill RAYMOND SLOYXNE, screams over and over again, for twenty-six minutes, from his bed, to which he's attached at the wrists and ankles by leather restraints, one question.

RAYMOND: Wanna play ball, Dad?

CURTAIN

Marty, wearing the same blue tuxedo he never returned after the therapy session in LA, clutched his partner's arm as he waited for applause—thunderous, life-affirming applause. While clutching, he whispered, quickly, into Milt's ear, "Listen, before people rush up here with movie offers for my play, remember, I'll pay you a flat fee for your help but I am not going to give you a percentage of the gross, so if you want to get lawyers involved . . . gentlemen, start your engines!"

One man clapped, but with one hand only, which he slammed against his skull several times because he had those implanted hearing aids stuck in the back of his head like prongs on the end of velvet VIP ropes and, in all likelihood, had heard none of Marty's words. The acting was solid, though a little rushed—Marty wrote that off to opening night jitters and promised to replace the actor playing Raymond, not just because he found his work disappointing but also because Marty had borrowed five dollars from him and didn't want to pay him back.

Milt tried to get the clapping started and succeeded to a point, but any enthusiasm faded after an usher told the few people who hadn't run like hell out of the theater to lift their feet so that she could "Mr. Clean the floor. You see, we get bad rats in here."

Milt and Marty and F.U.C.K. sat inside Sardi's on the night of the premiere, waiting, with great hope and anticipation, for the first reviews to come trickling in. When the kindest reviewer called the work "vomit," F.U.C.K. left without paying for her cannelloni. Marty, devastated, just sat there, mindlessly wrapping F.U.C.K.'s cannelloni in a cloth napkin to eat later.

"Vomit?" Marty asked of no one in particular.

A cranky waiter, passing by, heard the remark and shot back, "If it's vomit, why are you stealing one of our napkins to take it home in?"

Marty, blind with misdirected rage, lied to the waiter about having a dog at home "who just saved a busload of orphans from a fire! Is that okay with *you*, Mr. In-the-Country-Illegally?" The waiter replied that he was born in Cleveland and went about crumbing the table.

"Yeah, Cleveland, Puerto Rico!" the still wounded Marty snarled back, adding that "we oughta build a goddamn wall!"

Milt tried to buck Marty up by saying that the phrase "vomit" might draw "the current New York avant-garde-theater-going crowd, which I read somewhere is made up mostly of Wall Street yuppies who lead depraved secret night lives in pursuit of scatologically pornographic experiences and seventeen-year-old Goth runaways from the Midwest." He told Marty that he thought "vomit," the phrase itself, would make a great blurb on the theater's marquee—not to mention "on T-shirts that would sell like hotcakes in *Argosy* magazine"—as a reverse-psychology type of thing to draw people in, "here as we approach, ever more quickly, the end of the world. Which, in terms of the way your masterpiece has been so misunderstood, could not come fast enough for Mr. and Mrs. Theatergoer!"

Marty was touched by Milt's loyalty and told him that he'd reconsidered and would now give him a "small" piece of the play's movie sale money. "But not out of dollar one! Net profits only." And then, suddenly, his ego seized by the throat with anger, Marty decided not to sit back and just take it. He jumped to his feet, yanked the Al Hirschfeld celebrity caricature of Neil Simon off the wall at Sardi's, and ran out to the street with it, pledging to "find out where that know-nothing critic lives and shove it up his ass, glass frame and all!"

On the third subway they had to take to get to the critic's house, and with the drawing still on his lap, Marty obsessed to a now sleeping Milt about Neil Simon and the luck of the genetic draw. "How come Doc," he wanted to know, using Simon's nickname, "has been so fuckin' successful in the Business while his brother, Danny, who, in my opinion, was equally talented, didn't go as far?"

A toothless, fifty-eight-year-old homeless self-styled "student of the theater" sitting across from Milt and Marty on the train posited this thought. "Clearly Neil Simon experienced his childhood differently from older brother Danny, and that difference 'hurt him into art,' as John Keats said."

Milt and Marty exchanged looks; this was a pretty bright guy sitting over there. Marty felt a particular simpatico with the man for, clearly, his brilliance had obviously been as snubbed by the world as had Marty's. Marty took five dollars out of his pocket and instructed Milt to hand it to the homeless man. Milt took the money and started over but came right back.

"What's wrong?" Marty demanded.

"The guy reeks of his own excrement."

Marty told Milt to ignore that fact, as it did not undo "the wisdom gift he comes bearing to us." Milt held his nose, turned back around, and handed the guy the five bucks. This sage of the subway nodded appreciatively before continuing to bear some more wisdom.

"Take me, for example, gentlemen," he said. "As it just so happens I got all the talent in my family, which is why, at this very moment, I'm on my way to Cape Kennedy to be the first man ever to wear a Zorro costume in space." After a long pause Marty told Milt to go over to the guy and get his five dollars back.

The night was to end in still more disappointment, as the team never did find the house of the play's reviewer who had so savaged *Long Day's Journey into Nate.* So Marty had to be satisfied with stuffing the stolen Neil Simon drawing into the buttocks crack of the already vandalized Hans Christian Andersen statue in Central Park.

Unable to scale the heights of the "close-knit Jew-hating world of the legitimate stage," as Marty had come to experience it, Wagonman and Sloyxne were forced to return, tails between their respective legs, to Hollywood.

Gwen—and this was her "life gift," as Milt called it—forgave her husband for the "cruel, soul-killing thing you said about my meat loaf" and welcomed him home, but not before having to pay for Marty's plane ticket as well, which she could afford only by going to Sloyxne's filthy apartment and hocking his plain women pornography collection.

Once Milt and Marty were back in Hollywood, Bethany Mezner Roneth-Uffga, their longtime, age-old, now only sixty-eight-pound agent, tried like the devil herself to find work for her boys. But after fifty years in the business it seemed that word had creeped out on Milt and Marty. As Ms. Mezner Roneth-Uffga put it, "I hate to tell you this, my sweet babies, but you're officially considered piranhas in the industry!"

MARTY IS GOD

||||||||||||||||||||||||||||||

In direct and stupefying contrast to the fading of Wagonman and Sloyxne's never-ascending star, the careers of Leopold and Sand were lighting up the polluted skies of Tinseltown. Tom and Bob had climbed so high, so fast, that they soon began entertaining thoughts of a personal life.

Herbert "Herkie" Stengle, an old friend of Tom's from Miami, set him up with happiness one night. Tom nearly didn't go on the blind date because his favorite film, *Zorba the Greek*, was scheduled to be on TV that night and he was determined to watch it then, not tape it. Herkie, like Tom, had followed his dream out to Los Angeles and had become a very successful dress manufacturer after designing a ready-to-wear dress called Le Frock Sponge du Tahiti ("the Sponge Dress from Tahiti"), a day dress made (from endangered Tahitian sea sponge) for women who perspired through "land fabric." The dress doubled as a chamois cloth that could be used to wash down swamp boats in the Everglades. Herkie happened to work with a beautiful young blonde named Barbara Hauptman, who's dream it was to "marry a nice guy with a lot of money." How could Tom have known that on this very night, his future wife would be looking up at him through the most beautiful blue eyes ever seen in a Mafia-owned restaurant?

In Barbara, Tom was sure he'd found his life mate, the mother of his children, and the woman who would help him with math and spelling for the rest of his days.

The Leopold nuptials were held at Temple Ben Stein, the biggest shul ever built along the Wilshire corridor. Rabbi Shlomo Lopp, the show biz rabbi, as he billed himself, did twenty minutes before the vows about how Jack Nicholson got him courtside seats to the Lakers games. Never devoutly religious, Tom had agreed to visit Temple Ben Stein only after reacting badly to some Thai food and promising God that if he, Tom, would only stop throwing up he would give something back to his people. True to his word, Tom bought a sixty-inch three-color TV for the Ira and Tefka Schnadleman sanctuary of the synagogue, which freed Tom, in his heart, to then skip the next two years of Saturday services.

Bob, of course, honored Tom by being his best man, a favor happily returned shortly thereafter when Bob met and married Rose Udell. Rose was six inches taller than Bob, a fact that soon made her very impatient with him.

The Sand/Udell "meet cute," as pasty-skinned film buffs always call such encounters, also might never have taken place if Bob hadn't been in the market for a new blazer at his favorite big 'n' tall clothing shop called Jesus, Mister, What Happened to You? for Men. Having gained a good hundred pounds from all the congratulatory "Can you believe this, Tom, we've got a hit show!" dinners at Spago, Bob still cared every bit as much as he ever did about good tailoring. Another big boy who happened to be in Jesus, Mister . . . that day, shopping for cabana clothes, turned out to be Larry "the House" Perpich, whom Bob first met at the *Give Your Uncle Back His Legs* office at Paramount Studios on his and Tom's first day in the Business. Larry, who'd been a thirty-eight-year-old member of Norman Smalnitz's cadre of thirty-something wannabe-writer office gofers on that day, had risen through the show biz ranks to become the executive producer of his own series, *Hey Lard!*, which had lasted just two seasons on Fox before going into a lucrative syndication run in Latvia, where they need a minimum of thirty episodes in order to agree to run them forever. Larry was accompanied into Jesus, Mister . . . on that fateful day by his wife, Lorraine, a redhead of the terminally cute variety who, as it turned out, had a sister who taught fiction writing at a UCSB extension evening class. Bob made Lorraine laugh so hard while he was having his inseam measured she decided then and there to make him her brother-in-law.

While Lorraine was off paying for the four pairs of black ("They're so slimming on you, Larry!") 58-30 Dockers and two 5-X ("What fun birds, Larry!") parrot-patterned Hawaiian shirts and a set of cabana lounging clothes that Mighty Joe Young would feel good wearing at the hotel pool, Larry took Bob aside and whispered something to Bob that turned out to endear Larry to him forever. "Unlike Lorraine, Lorraine's sister is a good human being. If you hurt her, I'll track you down and fuck you in the ass." Although Bob found Larry's remark to be somewhat homoerotic in tone, he decided to accept it in the spirit in which, no doubt, Larry had meant it.

Bob wound up not only not hurting Lorraine's sister but proposing that very same night and having Rabbi Lopp perform their service. At Bob's wedding the show biz rabbi spoke for thirty-eight minutes about spending a Passover at music mogul Jerry Weintraub's villa on Lake Como and being asked to sing "Tradition" to the parents of Donnie and Marie Osmond, whom Mr. Weintraub hoped to convert to Judaism.

With bigger families come even bigger homes. Tom and Bob both purchased houses in a charming but not quite megasuccessful section of town called Brentwood. Tom fell in love with his place when the realtor told him Marilyn Monroe had overdosed next door, while Bob and Rose were sold on theirs after neighbors bragged about how Charles Manson had plans to kill them but had never gotten around to it.

Nine months after escrow closed, Tom and Barbara's first child, Olivia, was born, right there at home in their sumptuous lanai, with the help of ex–*Lost in Space* star Billy Mumy's birthing-coach wife. Bob and Rose, who were childless, celebrated Olivia's birth by dialing 1-800-LOVEISU and signing up to become the American parents of five different Sudanese orphans they'd "met" while watching a late-night TeleComPassion Industries "evangelistic infomercial" entitled "Could You Be My, Would You Be My, Won't You Be My Parent?" Because of the Sands' generous pledge of $18.50 a week for two years, the five aforementioned orphans would have chocolate milk—"or some nourishing equivalent thereof"—with every meal.

For the team of Leopold and Sand, the good times just kept coming! While their husbands worked day and night turning out variations of the same plot for *Wright for Each Other*, Barbara Leopold and Rose Sand busied themselves with charity work. Barbara founded W.W.F.B.A.T.H.C.T., or Wives Who Feel Bad About Their Housekeepers' Children's Teeth, a group that met one day a week at the Cheesecake Factory in Beverly Hills and made lists of dentists who would do pro bono gingivitis work for the kids of the people who took care of the women's kids so they could do charity work; meanwhile Rose drove LA's endless freeways each day buying bags of oranges from Mexican women along the road.

If running a hit show had allowed Tom and Bob the time to survey all that they had accomplished up until that point—to truly take it in, to assess all their blessings—the highlight of the whole magic carpet ride, besides good health and happy families and the quiet envy of the writers who worked for them, would have to have been the night Wolfgang Puck came out of his kitchen at Granita, his wonderful Malibu eatery, and delivered the news to the two men, who only twenty years earlier had been self-loathing children, that he was naming a salad after them: the "Tomcat Bobcat Salad," an honor Tom couldn't fully enjoy because it contained blue onions, which always made Leopold dream that his high school drama coach was chasing him with an ax and a copy of *Our Town*.

While Tom and Bob were enjoying such perks, as the latest toasts of the town, having undigestable salads named after them, Milt and Marty were barely holding on by their liver spots. For some reason, neither writer cared to think too much about the fact that Beth, their ancient, moth-weight agent, had been somehow owed a favor by someone in the porn industry, markers she was only too happy to call in so her two favorite—not to mention only—writers could have some walking-around money. Fearing that there might be a slight stigma attached to writing hard-core, occasionally anal-oriented adult entertainment, Milt and Marty decided to write under the names Murray Wagontan and No X. Sloyne. Amazingly, the very first porn flick they ever penned, *The Face Locker*, went on to win something called the Glass Clitoris Award, which was a trophy made entirely of Lucite. Except for the $2,500 the team split, 10 percent of which went to their agent and 29 percent to pay down their tab at the Cyclops, and aside from the perk of Marty contracting an infection from sitting on the set of *Toilet Teens*, writing porn just didn't get it for the team creatively. Writing gang bang scenarios or dialogue with "You like it, don't you? You like it when I do this!" simply wasn't comedy. In fact, there were moments, especially after Milt was enlisted as a "fluffer" on *Crack It to Her East of Splits*, when it all began to feel downright humiliating. Add to this career detour the fact that, in Marty's eyes anyway, Tom and Bob's good fortune seemed to rub his face in the "shit pile of my own career unfairness," and it's easy to see why Marty forced Milt to join him in a lawsuit against their onetime mentees, Tom Leopold and Bob Sand.

Milt and Marty's "moronically frivolous" lawsuit, as the judge, and even the judge's bailiff, characterized it, was based on the premise that the lead characters in *Wright for Each Other*—a beautiful young midwestern man and equally beautiful woman—were "based entirely on the real life personas" of one Milt Wagonman and Marty Sloyxne, two very Jewish men in their mid-seventies, who had never even been to the Midwest because, as Milt had declared in his deposition, "you can't get herring there."

The case would certainly have been tossed out of court on its own merits, but Marty's showing up on the first day of the proceedings in disguise, pretending to be his own attorney, absolutely infuriated the judge. The attorney Marty pretended to be was Big Jim Montgomery, a kindly, old Clarence Darrow–type with suspenders and a paper fan he waved back and forth across his face that had "Horton's Funeral Parlor" printed across it.

Being wronged by the courts only made Marty angrier with Tom and Bob for, in his madness, he believed that if those two "lucky pricks" had masqueraded as *their* own lawyers "the judge wouldn't've said boo about it!"

Finally, feeling as though the court system had let them down, Marty, and therefore Milt, had little choice but to stalk Tom and Bob to "give 'em a taste of their own medicine, godammit!" Milt couldn't understand how he and Marty were supposed to give them a taste of their own medicine when Tom and Bob had never been anything but nice to him and Marty. But Milt decided to disregard any negative thoughts he might have had about the stalking and just go with Marty on this one, for, after all, apart from a glitch here and there, hadn't Milt done pretty darn well in life following the lead of Mr. Marty Sloyxne? Why rock the boat?

Marty's first stalking began when he showed up, monumentally uninvited, at the birth of Tom's second child. Milt had pointed out the blessed event to him as seen in *Variety* and Marty decided to show up, feeling that even if his being there didn't work as a stalk, he could always "parlay it" into a sign of support . . . which is exactly what happened . . . sort of. To bluff his way into the Leopolds' delivery room, Marty stole some green surgical scrubs, a mask, a stethoscope, and for some unknown reason a proctosigmoidoscope. Milt got cold feet at the last minute and refused to follow Marty into the birthing room. Just going inside a hospital was hard for him after that time he'd been wheeled into the morgue instead of the recovery room following failed hernia operation number three. "No wonder," Milt thought at the time, "I couldn't get any of the other patients lying there to talk about the World Series."

Barbara Leopold had insisted she and Tom's second girl, Augusta, be born in a hospital after plans to enlarge the poolside lanai fell behind schedule when the immigration control people deported their entire team of "drywallers."

Marty was unmasked, literally, when Barbara's obstetrician asked Sloyxne to hand him a clamp and Marty replied, in full comic delivery, "I had the clap once but a *clamp* I never got!"

"Marty Sloyxne! What are you doing here!"

Marty was so taken aback by the genuineness of Tom and Barbara's protective parental instincts that all thoughts of his getting even with Tom for crimes not even he fully believed were ever committed against him dissolved and were instantly replaced, in what passed as Marty's heart, as genuine happiness at a new life being brought into the world. Marty tried to put a good face on the invasion. "I read about the blessed event child in *Variety*, or was it the *Reporter*, and just felt you'd want me here . . ."

"Get *out*!" Tom screamed, so loudly that Barbara's contractions ceased momentarily.

Marty held his ground. "Look, Leopold," Sloyxne spoke in measured tones. "All I'm doing here is showing you the support you never showed me and Milt by not hiring us on your hit show! Why should two wrongs not make a right vis-à-vis a little, defenseless newborn babe, not even in swaddling clothes yet, and who, I might add, never didn't hire me and Milt?"

A nurse called for security but Tom took matters into his own hands and led Marty out of the room just as their one-second-old child's head emerged. The doctor told Tom to turn back around so he wouldn't miss the sight. Tom did so and so did Marty, both marveling at nature's greatest but visually nauseating miracle. Tom ordered the old comedy writer out of the room once more. Marty, who had now been moved to the point of not hating Tom or anyone for a few minutes, had this to say: "What are you so mad at, for crissakes, Leopold? The fact that I looked inside your wife? This is no time to be thinking of your wife's genitals as sex objects, Tom! You sick fuck!"

Tom lost it at that and put the old man in a headlock, knocking off Marty's stolen surgical mask and making him drop his proctosigmoidoscope to the once-sterile floor. Out in the hall Tom was shocked to see Milt Wagonman standing there, holding up a congratulatory cigar for the "new papa!" Tom accepted the cigar with thanks, and then hated himself for it a moment later. Milt saw this softening of Leopold's demeanor as the perfect opportunity to offer himself and Marty as the baby's co-godfathers. To which Marty shouted at his partner, "What the hell's the matter with you, Milt? Jews don't have godfathers!"

Marty's heart stayed soft for three more days, after which it hardened enough for him and his resentment to camp out in a cheap Winnebago at the end of Bob Sand's driveway, where he showered, completely nude, with Bob's garden hose and accidentally ran over Bob and his wife Rose's pet bunny, Paladin. Filled almost instantly with remorse, Marty called Milt and insisted he meet him and the dead rabbit at the Cyclops to get roaring drunk. Once clobbered at the bar, Marty realized he hadn't really been stalking Tom and Bob in the classical manner at all; in other words, he wasn't stalking them out of hate but out of love! With one son confined to a mental institution, Marty had, he told himself, adopted the two young men, who, if only they got drunk enough, would be able to realize that they loved him, too. Milt agreed about the love stalking, but he was so drunk himself that he would have agreed to joining a cranberry lovers' club. Racked with guilt for maybe the very first time in his whole dreadful life, Marty decided then and there to make amends for the rabbit-killing misunderstanding by breaking into the Friars Club, the one from which the team had long ago been banned, and mixing the now-rotting bunny's carcass—which Milt had agreed to let him keep, encased in several layers of industrial-strength plastic wrap, inside the trunk of the Falcon—with the ashes inside the urn that housed the former Friars "Abbot and Dean Emeritus," the dearly beloved recovering alcoholic comedian named Joe E. Lewis. When asked by a Friars Club security guard, just before the man tasered Milt and Marty, "why would you put a dead rabbit in Mr. Lewis's urn?" Marty replied, "If the Egyptian pharaohs were buried with their favorite animals, why not the Great Joe E.?"

Maybe it was guilt over all their success, or maybe Tom and Bob still felt something for Milt and Marty—after all, the two old hacks *were* part of the lore associated with Leopold and Sand's comedy begin-nings—but the fact that Marty would feel bad enough about crushing a bunny's skull to open a forgotten old comedian's urn, and then get tasered for doing so, softened Tom's and Bob's hearts, and so they offered the team of Wagonman and Sloyxne jobs doing punch-up on *Wright for Each Other*. Truth is, the show practically ran itself by this point, anyway, so really, they said, how much damage could it do?

Thrilled to be out of butt fuck movies and back working "at the ol' yuk factory," as Marty christened this brand-new beginning, Milt thought it only appropriate he once again don his lucky pants for their very first day of work. Said pants, now resembling what a hobo might wear to his high school reunion, gave Milt, along with the cold meat loaf sandwiches Gwen packed him, the first day of school optimism he needed to face a room full of writers so young they didn't know who the hell Sammy Davis Jr. was.

Once on the job, and back in the room, Marty wasted no time pitching outdated jokes and slowing down the writing process with pointless and disgusting show biz stories, e.g., "They say Al Jolson liked to kill a colored kid every once in a while before he went on, cuz . . . y'know . . . it relaxed him." And that was just the story he told before his morning danish.

By lunch Marty had become absolutely smitten with Lucy Delle'bate, the supporting actress on the show who played Sally Den-tine. Marty mused, "I would drink day-old coffee from the natural ther-mos which is her round, firm, ghostly white ass and feel refreshed!" This he spoke over an open microphone during a tech rehearsal. Still, Tom and Bob stood by them through almost the entire first half of that first day, but even they had to admit defeat when, as Ms. Delle'bate napped, Marty snuck into her dressing room and painted the actress from head to toe in toxic gold paint—à la the old James Bond film *Goldfinger*.

Milt & Marty

Marty's "act of adoration . . . and adornment," as he called it, resulted in Lucy Delle'bate's near suffocation and an attempted murder charge being brought. All this before the stage manager even called "lunch!"

Tom and Bob pulled some strings with the LA Sheriff's Department (they had to promise to write a "jokey" version of *The Mikado* for the Police Benevolent Association) so that Marty only had to spend six weeks in jail. But "that's definitely *it!*" Leopold and Sand promised each other. Whatever debt they felt they owed the old-timers had been paid in full and then some. Neither man felt good about it but their agent made them take out a restraining order against Milt and Marty, something that hadn't been done since 1956 when Robert Young, Father in *Father Knows Best*, found Marty sleeping in the doghouse of his Bel Air estate.

Once released from confinement and cleared of any wrongdoing—in fact the charges were dropped when Marty was found to have a cholesterol count of 520 and it was determined that he'd never survive even a minimum-security prison term—Milt Wagonman commenced arranging the "best darned victory party any comedy writer ever threw any partner who'd ever been acquitted of almost painting someone to death." Milt, who'd mortgaged his home to pay the rent on Marty's $98.68-a-month apartment, was determined to run Marty the party he deserved, complete with pigs' knuckles, Marty's "nectarines of the Gods," and a merry band of his staunchest defenders, the people who'd stood by him "when the rest of the doggoned world was saying Martin Sloyxne was nothing but a never-was with severe and often dangerous delusions." The pigs' knuckles would be a cinch, Milt realized, but the loyal friends would be harder to find.

Then, in a rare burst of inventiveness, Milt decided he would try to talk his Polish cleaning lady into agreeing (for three hundred dollars, which was, at that time, approximately one-eighth of Milt and Gwen's net worth) to pretend, for Marty's benefit, that the crowd that would be gathered at the downtown LA Slavic Brethren Hall to celebrate her son Ivan's upcoming wedding (to the lovely Nishka Putski, the head cashier at the Gower Street Car Wash) had actually shown up to celebrate Marty's acquittal. Milt knew, and told his cleaning lady so, that if Marty ever became aware that not all of the Polish-speaking, completely drunken partygoers were there because of him, he would become "quite unpleasant, to say the least." To Milt's amazement, the cleaning lady agreed to perpetrate the fraud. To his further amazement, if Marty knew what was going on that day of the party/wedding he never let on. The "We Love Marty" bash went off without a hitch until Ivan, the son of Milt's cleaning lady, punched Marty in the face—hard—not only for leaping into the middle of a group of young unmarried women who'd been waiting to catch the bride's garter when she threw it their way backward, and with her eyes closed, but for licking and chewing and swallowing the garter after he'd caught it. Luckily for Ivan and his mother and his new bride and the 116 guests, Marty wasn't about to let anything—not even the broken orbital bone he suffered when Ivan hit him flush in the puss—tarnish the joy his freedom had brought him. He felt that he was loved, and the only proof he needed of that could be found in the reality of the presence of all those gathered around him—the people he cared about the most—complete strangers, who spoke not a word of English.

Two and a half days later, when the wedding was winding down and after most of the band had either thrown up, passed into alcohol-induced comas, or enjoyed illicit sex on the roof of the hall with one or more of the many sad married women attending the reception, Marty followed the wise-looking, unusually short, morbidly obese priest who'd married Ivan to Nishka outside for some air. And as both men stood on tiptoes, trying to catch a glimpse of the bride changing out of her gown and into her street clothes in the church rectory, Marty asked the holy man the question we all carry within us but fear the answer to. "Father, if you were in prison for, say, forty years, would you bang another man?"

The priest gave it some thought, for he found Marty to be a serious man, notwithstanding the moment an hour before when Marty had made the bride stand on his shoes as he waltzed her into the men's room.

"Why do you ask this, my son?" asked the priest.

"I ask it, Father," said Marty, "only to get it out of the way so that I can ask you the real question I wanted to ask you."

"Well, then," said the priest. "Ask it, because I gotta take a major leak." And then Marty bared what for anyone else would have been his soul. He said that show business wasn't giving him the kick it once had, and that "coming so close to losing it all, and being in jail with a bunch of tattooed non–show biz types" had opened his eyes to the possibility that there was more to life, more to the universe, than food or booze or banging a lot of plain-looking women. The priest agreed with Marty that there was, indeed, more to life than that which Marty had described, although he himself had never banged any kind of woman.

"Well, then," Marty asked, "how do you find life's meaning, for fuck sake?"

"I don't know," said the priest. "Do you like to draw?"

Marty told him that he sometimes liked to draw, and for the next forty minutes Marty and the priest sat down and drew that famous boxer dog that you always used to see on the back of that famous match book advertising that famous artists' school. Still, that wasn't doing it for Sloyxne. He grabbed the priest by his long, wedding cake–encrusted beard and ordered him to hand over the meaning of life. "Do it, Padre, tell me everything you know. Or I'll knee you so hard in the balls you'll never watch Bing Crosby in *Going My Way* again!"

"Look within, Martin!" said the priest.

"Within?" Martin repeated. "Where the hell's that?"

"Inside your soul, my son."

"Where's that?"

"In your heart of hearts."

"And where the fuck is that?"

"In your soul."

"You said that already."

Marty gave up and found the men's room and, while sitting on the can, had this thought—"Maybe I don't know what life's really all about because I don't believe in God"—which got interrupted when someone started knocking on his toilet stall. But Marty ignored the intrusive sound and kept on thinking. He was on to something and would have hated like hell to lose his thread. Yeah, he thought, maybe I made show business my God because (a) I wasn't that good in school and (b) nobody does God like the movies or television. Look at Claude Rains in *Here Comes Mr. Jordan* or James Mason in *Heaven Can Wait* with Warren Beatty. The pounding grew louder on the door of Marty's stall and he stayed silent until he could stay silent no longer.

"Fuck you, you insensitive motherfucker!" he shouted. "Can't you smell that I'm taking a shit, you dickwad?"

"Sorry, Mister," answered the sweet, trembling voice of a little girl. "I guess this is the wrong bathroom."

"That's okay, my darling," said Marty, semisweetly, before going back toward the path on which he was getting closest to his life-changing revelation. "Where was I?" he wondered. "Oh yeah . . . so if a guy as smart as I am—a guy who hasn't paid taxes in thirty years and never got caught for it—doesn't believe in God, then maybe, just maybe . . . the reason for that is because . . . I am . . ."

Another knock interrupted his journey toward the major revelation of his life. It was the little girl again, saying that she was right and Marty was wrong . . . that he was, indeed, crapping in the ladies' room. Marty told her to "please try the men's room, my darling, and let me get where I'm going." And then, even before the little girl had turned on her heels, he completed his thought, out loud. "Maybe, just maybe, I am God!" he said.

Hearing his voice—the voice of God?—utter the words shook him to his core. Sure, he'd always thought—even as far back as sand-lot sports, when he was always sixth to be picked for any team (by the way, wasn't 6 God's number?)—that he was smarter than any mortal man, but to possibly be God?

"How can you be God?" the little girl asked him as he completed the third, and most merciful, flush of his toilet. Marty hadn't realized, until that moment, that he had said out loud he might be God.

"Because if I'm not who is?" he shouted at her through the stall door. Marty always loved and relied on the wisdom of children, and so he waited for her response.

"I don't know, Mister," she answered, "but I just peed on my shoes."

Marty pulled up his pants and rushed out of the stall. The little girl, who was the sweetest little eight-year-old he had ever seen, nearly fainted at the stink that followed closely behind him.

"My goodness, Mister," she said. "What did you eat?"

Marty turned back around and answered her question as if he were speaking from a burning bush or someplace equally holy. "Pigs' knuckles, my child," he said. And then he rushed from the ladies' room without washing his hands.

Back out in the air Marty walked along the depressed, deprived downtown streets with a new perspective on his place in the world. Instead of laughing at or pushing the intrusive winos and homeless men and women away from him, as he usually did, he offered them each a dime. When a one-legged bag lady who was sitting in a provocative position on a stoop asked him for a dollar, Marty stopped, leaned down to her, grabbed hold of her stump, and shouted, "I command you to grow another leg!"

"What the fuck you doin', Captain?" shouted the delusional woman, the poorest of the poor.

Marty grabbed her stump more firmly and pointed it toward heaven, which revealed to him the fact that she was wearing men's underwear.

"Lord, heal this womanchild!" Marty cried out and then, remembering that back when he was pinching a loaf he had decided he was God, dropped her leg and walked on.

Marty waited for the people he passed to see his godliness, but they didn't. "There'll be plenty of time for that," he told himself. "Oh, yes . . . there will be plenty . . . of time . . . for that."

SLOYXNE-GRA-LA

||||||||||||||||||||||||||

If Bob had been a camel, which is the animal he would want to be if he could come back as an animal, Marty's gilding of Ms. Delle'bate would have been the straw that broke his back, for the negative personal dynamics that had been most troublingly alive in Bob's life, up to that point, finally boiled over when the sign WRIGHT FOR EACH OTHER PRODUCTION SUSPENDED UNTIL FURTHER NOTICE DUE TO ACTRESS PAINT POISONING was hung on the door to Stage 41.

Bob's wife, Rosie, announced, three days after Bob and Tom had heard that their recently shut down show had been nominated for five Emmy awards, including Best Sitcom, and four days after Lucy "she doesn't love gold" Delle'bate had been rushed to the Painted Character Actress Ward of Cedars Sinai hospital, that the Sand marriage was over.

"But why?" Bob kept wanting to know, worried, for one thing, among hundreds of others, that he might never again find anyone who not only knew how to make tapioca pudding from scratch but would be willing to let him eat it off her abdomen. "But why, Rosie? But why? But why?"

"Because, because, because," said Rosie, mocking Bob's repetitive interrogation. "I want to sit down."

"Sit down, my darling," said Bob.

"I want to be able to sit for five minutes," his wife repeated, not even close to verbatim, "and enjoy my own private time again, without having my life overwhelmed, twenty-four-seven, by Bob Sand's endless, unkillable constellation of needs, the most bizarre of which is that he keeps letting the abominable Marty Sloyxne back into our lives!"

"What does 'twenty-four-seven' mean?" asked Bob.

"It means every minute of every day," said Rose.

"Really? Wow. I've never heard it before."

"That's because it's never been said before, and that's because I just created it."

"You did?"

"Yes, Bob, I did! I'm creative too, you know!"

" 'Too'?" said Bob, trying desperately to keep Rosie the Human Dessert Plate in his life. "You're one of the most creative people I've ever known!"

"Too late," said Rosie.

"Too late for what?" asked Bob.

"For saying something for the first time that you should have been saying for years."

Bob, who usually ran to Tom and his wife, Barbara, when he was distraught, ran to Tom and his wife, Barbara. Tom and his wife, Barbara, who usually let Bob ramble on for hours when he was distraught, let him ramble on for hours.

"I shouldn't even be allowed outside by myself in public at this point in my life," said Bob, "much less be allowed to raise a child."

"A child?" said Tom's wife, Barbara, whom Tom had brought in, as if she were a member of the Level-headed Blue-eyed Shiksa Cavalry, to help him deal with what he knew would be a gut-sucking olympiad of pain. "But you don't have a child."

"Maybe not," says Bob, "but Rosie and I had been trying to have one for the past five hundred and forty-three days . . ."

"You counted the days," said Tom, in the calm tone of a man whose heart wasn't palpitating wildly, as it did every time, including this one, he found himself in the presence of someone even crazier than himself.

"I could've just said we'd been trying for a little more than eighteen months," said Bob, "but that wouldn't have done justice to the enormity of the emotional investment which all of a sudden looks like Rosie just threw right out the window."

"Oh," said Tom.

"Look on the bright side, Bob," said Barbara. "You and Rosie didn't get pregnant, which means that no innocent third party will be hurt."

"Maybe so," said Bob, "but do you have any idea how close she and I came to that not being the case? I mean, two totally immature individuals like us, who should've been held back in Pre-K till we were thirty? Can you grasp what a disaster it would've been for our poor kid if God had blessed us with children?"

"But don't you realize," asked Barbara, "how resilient kids—even imaginary ones—are?"

In the days following Lucy Delle'bate's being taken off the critical list, Bob wasn't the only one who had trouble concentrating on *You for Me and a Stew for You*, the *Wright for Each Other* spin-off pilot that he and Tom had been developing with the thought that Thelma Aloi, who played Glo, the fifty-something, even more man-hungry third banana best friend of Lucy's character on *Wright*, might star in it. Tom perceived the sudden interruption in what had been the steady forward movement of his and Bob's career as a forced retreat back to the bottom rung of the show biz ladder, and the fact that he had money in the bank and owned a home for the first time in his life did nothing to prevent Tom from an attack of multiple failure diseases—failure eczema, failure shingles, failure hemorrhoids, meager unemployment check failure cold sores, and a failure limp—which bore a shocking resemblance to the success diseases—success eczema, success shingles, success hemorrhoids, large residual check success cold sores, and a success limp—which his doctor had diagnosed shortly after *Wright* had gone on the air and which only "got a little better every day."

What had usually happened in the past, whenever Tom or Bob had experienced a sudden crisis in confidence, was that the partner not experiencing the crisis would take the one who was experiencing it out to lunch, where they would "talk it out." That both of them were now experiencing the same crisis in confidence made them decide to follow Tom's wife Barbara's suggestion they go and "talk things out" at lunch together, but that they go dutch.

The two partners went to a Venice Beach Strand café called the Fig Tree, which had been the place where they'd felt most comfortable, back in the days before they signed up for Norman Smalnitz's sitcom writing course, about sharing their show biz dreams—because every other desperate creative duo at every other table had been doing the same thing. On this day, however, it was the ruination of that dream on which Bob most wanted to expound.

"Tommy," he said, "I've come to the conclusion that our beloved business sucks as much as life does."

"Sorry, Bob! Wrong answer!" said Tom, in the voice of a game show emcee. "The correct answer is, It sucks for sure but not as much as life!"

"Don't do the game show voice, Tom."

"Fair enough," said Tom, morphing back into a guy who now had no answers, although he kept pitching. "But I think I know what's coming, man, and it's scaring the hell out of me. You're feeling down right now and for good reason. First our job gets put on hold till our actress can get herself unpainted and then your wife leaves you. But if I were you, I'd look on the bright side, which is that only one of those things is permanent."

"If you were me you'd feel the same way," said Bob.

"Bob, if I were you I would have killed myself a long time ago." Tom got a small smile out of him. "I know what you're saying, buddy, but I wouldn't think of leaving the Business, which is what I think you're thinking of doing, and *please* correct me if I'm wrong."

Bob said nothing.

"Case closed department," said Tom.

"My case is wide open," said Bob, "in terms of new life possibilities."

"Like what—working in a bookstore and hiding your face behind a copy of *Exodus* when one of the dinosaurs we worked with on *Give Your Uncle Back His Legs* walks in looking for a men's room?"

"I wasn't referring to career possibilities," said Bob.

"What other kind are there?"

"We came into the world as human beings—"

"Speak for yourself."

"—and we didn't start ignoring that till we got in the Business, where the last thing that matters is whether or not you're human. Every single comedy writer in history had an overriding personal issue they stopped working on when the Biz raised its ringed pinky finger and lured them into it."

"I was the kid who spent his days wishing he could fit into smaller-waisted chinos," said Tom.

When Tom finished admiring the poetry of what he had just said, Bob said, "It's not about you."

"I know that, Bobby. It's about Rosie leaving."

"Not really."

"No?"

"Not completely. I'm down about it, sure, but I'm more relieved than I am down."

"Oh, blow me!"

"I mean it," said Bob.

"Okay. It's about Rosie leaving combined with the show shutting down, then."

"No."

"What's it about, then? I want to order lunch," said Tom.

"It's about Marty."

"Marty?"

"As in Marty Sloyxne. Rosie thought the fact that I kept letting Marty back in my life was an indication that something was wrong with me," said Bob.

"Well, of course it is, but so what? Barbara thinks I'm insane for that reason, too, among many others, but you two took vows, for crying out loud!"

"Well, Rosie can't get past it. Maybe she's right, maybe in some sick way I love Marty more than my own wife."

Tom was stunned. "If you're going to keep talking like that, Bob, I may order the crabcakes, and you know what seafood does to me."

"Think about it, Tommy." Bob reached for a piece of bread but put it back, a sure sign to Tom that what he was about to say was serious. "The overriding personal issue of my life has always been that my father wasn't there for me."

"I thought your overriding issue was your mother abandoning you for a famous clown?"

"I was relieved when she left too."

"And Marty Sloyxne's a good surrogate?"

"He cares about me."

Tom paused for a beat, and then he called for the check.

"Look, Tom, just because Marty's chemically imbalanced and self-involved doesn't mean he's not caring," said Bob, looking very much to Tom like he believed all this bullshit. "I believe Marty cares about Milt, and I believe he cares about you too, Tom."

"He cares about pastrami."

"I believe Marty lives by a code."

"Bob, you're scaring me now."

"I'm serious, man. He is always himself. He's always Marty, and he never pretends to be anyone else."

"Listen, man, with all due respect, your father pretends to be an Indian chief, and anybody would look good after that."

Bob took that in. "You may have a point," he said, and then he said, "Do you know who created the phrase 'twenty-four-seven,' by the way?"

"Marty?"

"No. Rosie."

Before Tom had a chance to say that he had heard the phrase and that it was said by many, many people, a twinkle-eyed, beatifically smiling teenager in her mid-forties—a heartbroken, life-beaten West LA veteran of bad drugs and bad clothes—approached their table, pressing one long, tanned index finger against her pursed lips, handed each of them a tangerine-toned one-sheet flyer emblazoned with the purple words: "Don't You Think You've Said Enough?," and then turned and disappeared back out onto the Strand.

" 'No life on Mars' my ass," said Tom, which made both of them laugh until they started reading their respective copy of the brochure to themselves.

"Holy shit," murmured Tom, his face suddenly devoid of color. "Speak of the devil."

" 'Don't you think you've said enough?' " read Bob out loud. " 'Might the cause of your overwhelming feelings of disconnectedness and ineffectiveness and frustration and rage be the millions upon millions of words you've spoken to others and heard others speak to you—words which have done nobody—neither you, nor them, nor anyone else in the world, nor the world, itself—any good whatsoever?' "

" 'Don't you think you've heard enough?' " continued Tom. " 'And talked enough? And had enough? Consider the possibility that M. Ron Sloyxne's Silentexology, the foundation of which is built on four simple words—'Shut the Fuck Up!'—may be the only real alternative, for you, to an empty, meaningless life. The Church of Silentexology, founded by M. Ron Sloyxne just a few short weeks ago, has already attracted thousands to its altar and changed thousands of lives for the better. M. Ron Sloyxne's Church of Silentexology, located on the breathtakingly beautiful grounds of Sloyxne-gra-la, within loving distance of the Pacific Ocean, P.O. Box 7777777, Big Sur, California. Telephone: 415-SILENCE.' "

Bob noticed when Tom looked up from the flyer that his pallor was even a ghostlier white than usual.

"Do you think it's him?" asked Tom.

"Absolutely."

"Why?"

"Who else would it be?"

Bob shook his head, put his bread down, picked up the Silentexology brochure again, quickly discarded it for the bread once more, then said, "Forget everything I said, man. I had no idea how delusional the poor guy really was." But Bob didn't eat the bread . . . and that concerned his old friend.

Fortunately, with no actual show to produce, there were ninety-six phone messages for Tom and Bob to busy themselves with. Repairing to their respective offices, they each sifted through forty-eight of them from various agents and subagents and others who were eager to send the boys spec scripts from their clients, featured actors and actresses who were either in the permanent cast of *Wright for Each Other*, or had done guests shots on the show, or had auditioned to do guest shots on the show but hadn't yet heard back from the casting people, or had just arrived in LA from the Midwest where they'd appeared in "various high school productions" of *Fiddler on the Roof* and wanted to know if there was any way that the producers of "my all-time favorite show!" could help get them jobs as extras on one of the upcoming episodes so they wouldn't have to tell friends and family they were wrong to believe in their talent. Tom was surprised and slightly sickened to see that Message 61 was Milt Wagonman's wife, Gwen: "My husband believes that it is his mission in life to go and try to save his psychotic partner, who has started a religion in Big Sur, from himself. You are the only people in the world, other than me and that psycho, whose opinion he respects, and I need your help in trying to dissuade Milton from ruining our marriage, which is what will happen if he goes through with his mission. I am sorry to intrude on your lives but I am the desperate wife of a fellow comedy writer."

Over in his office, Bob was getting more and more depressed by the tsunami of human yearning that rose up from those "While You Were Out" message sheets. He sat back in his chair, threw his feet up on his desk, grabbed his remote from the top drawer, pointed it at his studio-provided twenty-seven-inch television set, clicked it on to an afternoon show called *Those Were the Days*, and started watching the footage of President Nixon's good-bye speech delivered from the Oval Office in 1974.

"Holy shit," mumbled Bob, as the gist of what Nixon had said began to sink in. He jumped up, dashed down the hall, stuck his head in Tom's office, and asked, "Can you believe Nixon was that eloquent when he left?"

"When he left what?" asked Tom.

"The presidency."

"That was some time ago, wasn't it, Bob?" asked Tom in his psychiatrist voice. "By the way, I just spoke to the hospital and Lucy's doing better. They got her color down to a 'tasteful rose gold with deep bronze lusters.'"

"That's good news," said Bob, who then immediately returned to his own inner Nixon tapes.

"Say what you want about the man, he had the balls to just up and walk out on his life, y'know?"

"They were going to throw him out of his life anyway, weren't they?" asked Tom. "I mean, I'm no historian, but . . ."

Bob picked up Tom's remote, pointed it at his studio-provided twenty-seven-inch color TV, and clicked it on.

"I remember my old man," said the perspiring, misty-eyed Nixon. "I think that they would have called him sort of a little man, common man. He didn't consider himself that way,"

"Holy shit," said Bob. "He's saying good-bye to the country!"

"He *said* it already, Bob."

"Nobody will ever write a book, probably, about my mother," said Nixon on the screen. "Well, I guess all of you would say this about your mother—my mother was a saint. Yes, she will have no books written about her. But she was a saint."

"My mother was kind of a saint before she walked out on me," Bob whispered.

"What little you've said about her sounded very nice," Tom remarked respectfully.

"I wonder how's she's doing out in the world . . ."

Before Tom could say "I'm sure she's doing great!" Bob was back in his own office.

Tom went back and forth with himself about whether or not to tell his partner about Gwen's message. He finally decided against it, fearing that in his current state Bob just couldn't handle anymore Milt and Marty madness. After all, there was a moment back at lunch when he'd seen his partner go dangerously pro-Sloyxne.

Bob stayed planted in his chair for nine hours after Tom had left the office for the day before deciding, finally, to seek help from a higher power.

After walking west for several hours, Bob reached the Pacific Coast Highway just as the sun was coming up and took thirty seconds to ingest the delicious pink-orange-lavender-powder blue one-of-a-kind beauty of it all before sticking out his thumb and hitching northward. After forty minutes he found his ride.

"Who you running away from, hon?"

"Good question."

"Where you headed?"

"Big Sur."

"That's my place."

"Do you live there?"

"No, baby," she said. "I just keep my heart there. My name's Marti, with an 'i.' What's yours?"

"Bob, with a B-o-b," said Bob, stunned by the cosmic coincidence that of all the girls' names available on earth the one belonging to the one person in three billion who had stopped to pick him up was "Marti."

"Well, hop in my rig, Bob with a B-o-b, and I'll take you where you're g-o-i-n apostrophe."

She couldn't have been more than seventy-five, as Bob remembers her, but she had the body of a well-preserved sixty and the wise demeanor of a woman at least five times that age. She was wearing white silver-tasseled cowgirl boots, a short-short denim skirt, and a matching pearl-buttoned shirt (and it didn't hurt, either, that she smelled like soap and looked at him through ageless robin's-egg-blue eyes with navy blue borders and wore a black Cleopatra wig above multiple layers of moist Caribbean Coral lipsticked lips and had the kind of freakishly healthy-looking teeth that would've caused a coroner, if he'd had to estimate the age of the corpse they were attached to using only the teeth as his guide, to guess "twenty"). Bob watched Marti grip the steering wheel of her eighteen-wheeler with her thick, sturdy, no-nonsense farmgirl hands as upbeat guitar music, country style, filled her cab.

"Nice music," said Bob.

"That's Scotty Moore, baby."

"Who's he?"

"The greatest man who ever lived, and not a bad little guitarist, either."

She told Bob that she was a native of Conroe, Texas, and that she'd run away from home, "which was, unlike Disneyland, not the happiest place on earth," when she was sixteen; that she'd been "adopted, a lifetime ago" by truckers, "the greatest human beings, pound-for-pound, in the world," who'd taught her how to drive eighteen-wheelers; that she'd met Scotty Moore, Elvis Presley's guitar player, back in Memphis in 1956 and that it was there and then that he became her "second Daddy, but the only good one," even though he was twenty-four, at the time, and she was forty, "but only in terms of years . . . in terms of maturity I was seven"; that she "lock, stock, and barrel" owned the big rig Bob was riding in; and that she'd been "minding my own business, hauling apricots from San Diego to British Columbia, as has been my habit, these days" when she spotted him—or, as she described him, "the most vulnerable, heartbreaking mound of little sad-eyed fat boy" she thought she'd ever seen.

"I can tell you this right now, hon," she said, less than ten minutes into their journey. "I love you very deeply, and I want you even more, and if you don't feel that way about me I'd appreciate it very much if you'd say so right now so's I can pull this rig over and let you out and begin the heartbreaking process of forgettin' I ever saw your beautiful little self."

"No," said Bob, meaning what he was about to say with all his confused heart. "I feel the same way about you."

Somewhere up the coast, on a lonely stretch of highway between Santa Barbara and San Luis Obispo, Marti pulled her rig off the road and into a field of high weeds, at which time she and Bob repaired rearward from her cab to the only real home she said she'd ever known—a wonderland of red neon replete with ceiling mirrors, a rotating dance light, an incensed-and-candled shrine to Scotty Moore, and a circular king-sized bed covered in big game pelts.

"How old are you, Bob?" she asked.

"Thirty-four, Marti."

"I'm seventy-three, hon," she said, "which means that I was thirty-nine when you were born, which means—"

"The only thing that means anything," said Bob, "is that you're beautiful," which caused Marti to fling herself backward onto what were obviously soon to be her and Bob's love pelts as her big silent tears rolled over the surface of her dense not particularly well applied pancake makeup.

Bob was right there, with the elderly yet well-preserved woman's heart and world and love, his for the asking, but then, just as his lips got close to hers, the face of the other Marty in his life, the one who spelled his name with a "y," appeared as if through some insidious, otherworldly conspiracy on top of her face, so that for him to kiss her would have been for him to kiss him. And so Bob jumped backward and ran at full speed back into her cab and out her passenger door and down into the high weeds of the anonymous field, through which he galloped until he was once again on the highway, where he immediately caught another ride headed north, hoping against hope that he would not be forever debilitated sexually by his memory of—and strange love for—his Marti with an "i."

The first thing Bob wanted to know when he laid eyes on the modest, less than magnificent sprawl of parched, more-inland-than-oceanfront acreage which was Sloyxne-gra-la for the first time was, "How the hell did he do it?" He wanted to know how, in three weeks' time, the virtually penniless Marty Sloyxne had been able to go from actress painter and confirmed television comedy thief to CEO of a new religious order, the tenets of which were being practiced (as Bob stood there, mouth agape, on that fateful late afternoon at the base of that less than magnificent property) inside three run-down buildings made of what even he, who knew nothing about the construction industry, knew were less than highest-quality metals, woods, and panes of glass.

The second thing he wanted to know was why the big tangerine-toned twelve-year-old limousine, the sides of which were emblazoned with purple-toned letters asking the question "Don't You Think You've Said Enough?," was bearing down on him from the top of the hill at what seemed to be a recklessly high rate of speed. The limo came screeching to a halt at his feet and regurgitated the completely bald driver, a muscular Viking-lost-in-the-modern-world Swedish type of individual, who looked in his tangerine-toned jumpsuit to be in his early twenties, before he could bend down and pick up his rapidly beating heart from the perfectly manicured grass. The driver took hold of Bob's arm, guided him to the limo's passenger door, and implored him, without saying a word, to enter the vehicle.

By the time the big Viking had taken his place behind the wheel Bob hadn't yet finished sinking down into the cracking, sun-damaged leather of his seat. His thought, at that moment, as strange as it was even for him, was that he now knew how it felt to be hugged from behind by Weezy from *The Jeffersons*.

The Viking made a U-turn on the grass and headed back up the hill at a ridiculous speed, past the worn-out buildings and into the woods along a kidney-damaging bumpy dirt road that seemed, from the angle in which it placed the limo, headed for the sky. After a good ten minutes the bumpy dirt road became a slightly less damaged cement one, and the vehicle seemed to stay earthbound. In the distance, through the trees, Bob could see a small white tent festooned with twenty or so tiny white stringed lights—half of which worked—that offered very little of that which someone from any affluent LA neighborhood would call illumination. Bob knew immediately that this was where Marty Sloyxne lived.

"Where am I going?" Bob asked the driver, who handed him a tangerine-toned index card emblazoned with purple-toned letters reading, "Don't You Think You've Asked Enough Questions?"

The only thing tentlike about the small tent was its exterior canvas. Its interior was a depressingly meager home-office complex with three pieces of unpainted furniture and fake wood flooring.

Bob was guided by the Viking into a corner of the tent where he underwent a wordless strip search, which seemed to amuse the Viking but was traumatic for Bob because he'd never even seen himself naked. After the search, the Viking picked Bob's clothes up from the floor, flung them at him, pointed to the unpainted wooden chair in the corner, threw a pair of earphones at him, and left the room. The moment Bob had settled into the chair and attached the earphones to his head, the taped voice of Marty (who now called himself M. Ron, and whose "x" may or may not, in its new incarnation, have remained silent) Sloyxne intoned, "Congratulations on your instincts. The fact that you're here means that you know, deep down, that you should be here. Now, since you must have at least begun considering the possibility that you may very well have said enough in your life, all you have to do is shut the fuck up."

With that, the door opened and M. Ron Sloyxne, looking God-like—what with his normally dry, long, and wild hair having been styled and pomaded and tamed back into a quintessential John Forsythe slickness, and his chubby body luxuriating in a flowing purple-toned robe with tangerine-toned piping, and accompanied by three leggy teenaged bleached-blonde triplets in tangerine-toned bikinis with purple-toned piping—entered the room, stood at its center with his arms folded, and looked Bob in the eye.

"Hello, Marty," said Bob.

The triplets gasped as one.

"Who are you?" M. Ron Sloyxne wanted to know.

"Come on, man," said Bob. "It's me. Bob. Bob Sand!"

" 'Marty' is my slave name," said Marty.

"What are you talking about?" asked Bob. "We worked together on *Give Your Uncle Back His Legs*! You took me and Tom Leopold on a safari to see Milton Berle's penis on our first day in show business! Don't you remember?"

"After slaves liberate themselves," said M. Ron Sloyxne, "they don't remember the people they wrote comedy with while they were slaves. Why are you here?"

"To ask you a question."

"You have five seconds."

"Okay . . . uhhh . . . could I ask you two of them?"

"You have ten seconds."

"Great. Question one. Where the hell did you get the money to start your church?"

M. Ron Sloyxne turned to his adorable, clingy triplet bath maidens and said, "Father needs a private moment, my babies."

"Yes, Father," said the three girls, who then left the room.

"They call you Father, huh?" said Bob.

"Is that your second question?"

"No. Forget I asked it."

"The funds necessary to make the idea of Silentexology a reality were provided by an old friend of mine from New York," said M. Ron Sloyxne.

"A rich old friend, no doubt."

"I suppose so, yes."

"And she was a woman, I bet."

M. Ron Sloyxne smiled Marty Sloyxne's smile as he said, "Her professional name, whilst she was working as a chorus girl at my old pal Lou 'Father of Barbara' Walters's magnificent Latin Quarter in New York, was Vivian St. Vavavoom, but I knew her, back when I was bangin' her older sister in the Bronx during my high school days, as Helene Schneck. Anyways, she married a billionaire—some hyperdriven almost but not quite a midget prick who owned the worldwide rights to the word 'maybe,' or some shit like that—who choked on a Cornish game hen bone at the 21 Club in his eighty-eighth year of life on earth and left her everything. After the embarrassing failure of my misunderstood masterpiece *Long Day's Journey into Nate*—what with needing a place to stay and a woman to be held by whilst engaged in the process of rebuilding my life—I gave Helene a holler and she let me back into her life. The idea for the church was hers. It came to her in the middle of our fourteenth shared glass of a wonderful Oregon pinot gris she had flown in every month from the Pacific Northwest, where she owned most of Portland. Lucky for me, she was easily as lost as I was, in the spiritual sense, and, being that she'd always been enamored of what she called the hidden, untapped power of my mystical side, the rest, good sir, is Silentexology."

Tom was awakened at four a.m. the next morning by the ringing of his phone.

"Hello?"

"Tommy?"

"Who is this?"

"Me. Milt."

"Jesus, Milt, do you know what time it is?"

"Yes, I certainly do."

"It's four a.m., man."

"I know that and I'm deeply sorry. Though I have nothing against the predawn itself . . . I've always found it a good time to reflect—"

"Why are you calling me, Milt?"

"Because," Wagonman said. "Your partner is in trouble."

"You mean *your* partner is."

"No, I mean *our* partner is."

"I think you're confused, Milt. I got a phone message from your wife that said that Marty had lost his mind and started a religion and that you were going to go up there and break it up."

156

"Wow. Gwen actually said all of that?" Milt was impressed. "I'm lucky if I can get one Post-It note out of the woman with 'C-U-Later' on it. Anyhoo, you and me need to go up to Big Sur and deprogram—I think that's what they call it—the both of 'em."

Tom, who regretted his decision to go with Milt long before the jet's wheels left the ground, had to keep reminding himself, as the reality of what he was doing and where he was going got absorbed deeper and deeper into his conscious mind, that his partner was worth saving, even if Milt's was not. He perceived Bob and himself—the way they'd risked everything to come to LA, the way they'd then made a career out of nothing—as two army buddies who had been able to take a beach called show biz on nothing but the D-day of their talent, thereby forging an unbreakable bond that nothing could destroy. Tom made a mental note to use the "had been able to take a beach called show biz on the D-day of our talent" line in a novel he might write if it wound up all the show biz money dried up.

Milt, who was a nervous flier, steadied himself by telling Tom several cute stories, beginning with one of the myths that had grown up around the Wagonman and Sloyxne partnership, which was an apocryphal tale of Marty's eating the ring finger and wedding ring off a Chinese delivery boy's hand after a particularly bad sitcom pilot run-through.

"But people have blown that story way the heck out of proportion," said Milt. "Martin never ate the kid's whole finger, as has been reported, plus he eventually fished the ring, which he did happen to swallow that day, out of his terlet and gave it back."

"I'm glad you cleared that up," said Tom, "'cause I'd always heard—"

"I know what you heard," said Milt, "but I was there, and there is never an iota of truth in any fact."

"Good point."

"What happened was, it was two in the morning, and we were trying to patch story holes in *My Mother the Chihuahua*, and the doggoned network told us, at the last minute, that we had to make it a workplace comedy. It tore the heart out of the piece, but hey . . . it's their football, right? So we had to go along. Marty, as per usual, was more upset about it than I was, and so when the delivery kid forgot to bring the duck sauce Marty jumped him and ate two-thirds of his finger off. I pace when I'm upset and Marty eats people's fingers. Everybody's different, so be it."

Milt couldn't help but laugh at the memory of it, and he continued laughing until his and Tom's plane hit some turbulence, at which point the older man crapped in his pants. Humiliated, Milt forced himself to ask Tom if he would please help him change his trousers, as he had taken so much Dramamine he wasn't sure he could handle the task alone. The two men got some pretty nasty looks as they walked up the aisle, and the looks got nastier as the lookers started getting more of a whiff.

Once they had made it to the bathroom Tom couldn't believe that so much shit could come out of one human being. *It's like shit from 1954*, he thought to himself. After stuffing the offended trousers in the lavatory's trash bin, Tom started helping Milt into his emergency pair of trousers, and it was then that he couldn't help but notice a large scar that ran the length of Milt's lower back. When Milt saw him looking at the scar, he snapped. "That's just a gallbladder scar! Marty never had one of my kidneys stolen to pay off some gambling debts, awright? Never!"

Tom had never seen Milt act so defensively and muttered something about how tough those gallbladder operations could be. The ferocity of his outburst made Milt void anew into his emergency pants. Not a huge amount this time, fortunately, but still enough to make rows 12 through 18 have to live with the stultifying results.

Milt & Marty

"In all the years you've known Marty," Tom asked, trying not to keep the fact that the anger being leveled at them from the other passengers was becoming palpable, "did you ever get any indication from the guy that he might one day start a religion?"

He had posed the question gingerly, wanting to step lightly after sensing that Milt wanted very much to open his heart but that he also had an intense desire to finish his airline peanuts.

"Nothing about my partner . . . and you'll notice, Tommy, I don't say ex-partner . . . would surprise me. Did you know, for example, that Martin once masturbated Lee Marvin?"

"Really?"

"Hand to God!" he said, before apologizing for saying the word "masturbated." After which he continued, "Mr. Marvin was filming the interiors for *The Klansman*, a flop that was supposed to star, I think, Richard Harris, the actor who starred in *A Man Called Horse*, and . . . remember that scene, by the way, when Harris, who wanted to be an Indian, was hung from a tree by his nipples?"

Tom remarked that he'd always thought that scene was one of the truest moments in the history of film, but Milt didn't hear him, as he was busy apologizing for having said "hung by his nipples."

"Marty and I were consulting on *Waffles and Syrup*," said Milt, "which had the very first all-black cast on a three-camera show. That's what the schvartzes called themselves, back then, by the way—blacks, not Negroes. But Marty could never remember what the most current politically correct appellation of the moment was for that particular ethnic group, and so he called everybody in the cast—as well as fifty-one percent of the writing staff and fifty-one percent of the crew—'coloreds,' which they all hated equally, except for this one actor, Jerome 'Pigfeet' Johnson, who played Uncle Cleophus, who hated the word the most and tried to stab Marty in the eye with an Afro comb."

"My God!" said Tom.

"May I finish, please?" asked the rarely impatient Milt.

"Of course," said Tom. "Forgive me, please."

"Forgiveness given. And so Marty and I are on lunch break, see, and so we walk by Marvin's dressing room and see that the door's open, and we peek in and there he is, lying naked as a jaybird on a massage table with a washcloth over his eyes, yelling for the Swedish masseuse, who he don't know has left the room, okay? 'Start the fuckin' massage, Inga!' he yells. 'I haven't got all fuckin' day!' So Marty gives me a wink and puts on his girly voice and asks Lee if he prefers deep tissue or Swedish. He says, 'Swedish, as always!' and Marty begins massaging him. Now keep in mind, Tommy, that this is the man who, for my money, is the toughest villain in moviedom, and he's lying there naked with a common washcloth still over his eyes, right? So two seconds in Marty starts, y'know, j-ing him off, as they say, and Marvin, believing Marty to be a knockout Nordic babe, lets my partner, y'know, give him a happy ending. There was nothing homosexual about the act, okay?"

"Of course there wasn't."

"I mean it."

"I know you do."

"Not one iota of queerness about it, understand me, son?"

"Certainly."

"Marty just wanted to have a good story to tell the other writers back in the room, and there was no way the guys wouldn't believe him, 'cause Lee had 'Cat Ballou'ed all over Marty's beloved maroon Members Only jacket."

The memory turned Milt wistful. His eyes filled with tears.

Over some of the smallest airline pretzels Tom had ever forced down, the conversation lost some of its lightheartedness. Milt conceded that even though Marty had replaced him with a cause as noble as religion, he had still been replaced, and that was something that cut deep.

After picking up their rental car—a purple-and-white AMC Gremlin, the interior of which smelled like a cheese wheel stored in Barry White's cabana clothes—Tom asked Milt how a lame story like Marty selling his kidney ever even got started. He knew that it was foolhardy to ask such a thing of the man, but he couldn't stop himself. Gallbladder scars were usually on the front, after all, and something about Milt's reaction told Tom there was more to the story. Milt ignored the question, choosing instead to thank Tom for lending him his bicycle pants, "which in truth make my keester look rounder than either my original or my emergency pants."

Milt filled the next hour of the drive north by telling Tom a cute story about Marty and Milt's daughter, Randi.

"It was the very first Take Your Daughter to Work Day and, having no daughter of his own, we were glad to let Marty take Randi along with him down to the men's room of the Roosevelt Hotel where he was moonlighting as an attendant. Our Randi sat there in the john that whole day with Marty until his relief showed up, you should pardon the expression," Milt said wistfully. "She helped Marty with towels and the pouring of Vitalis and the replacing of urinal cakes, which is fun for a kid, and counting the tips in his jar, while men came in and out all day and did their ablutions. My point, Tommy, is that Marty is family!"

A mechanical nod was absolutely all Tom could muster.

Several hours later, as they pulled into the driveway that led to Sloyxne-gra-la, Milt was transfixed by what only he and he alone would perceive as "the lush expanse of the place," while Tom became transfixed by the four nearly identical-looking women picketing outside the gates.

"Who are they?" wondered Tom, studying the women's home-made picket signs which read . . .

"F.W.O.M.S.U.s," said Milt.

"Who are F.W.O.M.S.U.s?"

"Former Wives of Marty Sloyxne United."

"They have a club?"

"This must be the West Coast branch. It's a nationally sanctioned union. Their dental plan is forgetaboutit!" said Milt.

"Why do you think they're picketing?"

"He was probably less than diligent alimony-wise."

The four women, who held signs reading "We Are Not Marty Sloyxne's Silent Exes!," blocked the car but Milt, who had known them all, shoved the vehicle in park, got out, and said hello.

"Hi, Marilyn, Marilyn, Marilyn, and Marilyn," he said. "It's me. Milt."

The women, who were glad to see him, shrieked and dropped their signs and hugged him before picking their signs back up and stepping aside to make room for the rental car to move through the gates.

"They're all four named Marilyn?" asked Tom, after Milt had reentered the car.

"All *nine* of his wives were named Marilyn," said Milt. "If they weren't named Marilyn when he met 'em, he made 'em change it as a condition of the wedding. He tied the knot nine times between January 1, 1950, and December 31, 1989—and after the ninth one failed he never married again. I knew all nine of his wives, and I can't to this day tell you which one was sweeter or kinder or nicer or better for the guy than any of the others. They were all wonderful people, in my opinion, and they all adored him the way Fay Wray probably would've wound up adoring Kong if that pain in the neck Robert Armstrong had only let her stay on Kong Island. 'My adorable little treasure,' Marty would call whichever woman he happened to be married to at the time, and every time he did that you'd hold your breath and think, Well, whaddya know? Maybe he's finally growing up, maybe he's learned, after all this time, what's really important in life. But then he'd say something like—and please forgive my French—'And she swallows my frightful hog like a fuckin' Eureka Zoom Canister Powersuck 4000' or some such private thing and the moment would be all but ruined."

As Milt looked around the grounds he seemed preoccupied. "Looks like my partner has moved on," he said. "Looks like he's moved right on, right past his old pal Milt Wagonman."

Suddenly, Tom and Milt spotted two men, one much older than the other, waving their hands madly and running, as fast as they could, down the road toward the rental car. Tom soon realized that the two desperate men were Marty Sloyxne and Bob Sand! As Milt slowed the car, Tom could hear Marty scream, "Don't turn the fuckin' engine off, boychik!" before throwing himself through the open rear window and onto the backseat. Bob followed him in but not before slamming the ribs on the right side of his body on the door rim.

"Turn the car around and get us the hell outa here now!" shouted Marty.

"Not too fast!" gasped Bob. "My side caved in!"

When Tom finally stopped gawking through the rearview mirror at his and Milt's crazy partners, he moved his eyeballs just enough to catch sight of an angry mini-mob of six torch-bearing human beings barreling down on them from the rear.

"Who the hell are the people with the goddamned torches?" asked Tom.

Marty said that they were "the idiots who didn't like the poison cream soda I offered 'em!" And then he expelled a maniacal "Baaaa-waaaaahhhh!" of a laugh, got on his hands and knees, undid and dropped his pants, backed up to the open rear window, and mooned the six angry torch bearers who, Tom later found out, had made up more than half of the entire membership roster of Marty's former followers.

"What do they want?" asked Milt.

"My blood," said Marty.

"Why?"

" 'Cause they devoted their lives, for no apparent good reason, to Silentexology, a religion that failed, and to a religious leader who failed *them*!"

As the rental Gremlin left the torch bearers in the dust, Marty stuck his head out the window and shouted, "Ya gullible little need-a-daddy jerkoffs ya!"

Tom gazed at the rearview and took one last look at the mob, which reminded him of the angry townsfolk who had chased down the Frankenstein monster, growing smaller in the distance behind him. Turning right onto the Pacific Coast Highway, Tom was able to see that he and his passengers were not yet home free, for a quartet of ex-Silentexologists in a Sloyxne-gra-la golf cart (tangerine-toned, with purple-toned piping) had pulled their little vehicle close enough to the Gremlin for the four of them to reach out and grab onto the car's rear bumper. Tom stuck his head out the window as he sped up, hoping to shout them off, but the words caught in his throat when he realized that the four diehards were Willie Nelson, Tiger Woods, Julia Roberts, and Roy Campanella, whom Tom had thought he'd seen just a few moments earlier—before dismissing the thought as a hallucination—being pushed in his wheelchair by a galloping Ms. Roberts. The four cart-riding ex-Silentexolgists were obviously furious, and Campy was yelling, "You come into *my* house under false Milton Berle's cock pretenses, Marty, and this is how you treat me?"

When they were safely away after a couple of "Steve McQueen Is Bullitt!" stops and starts, which had successfully dislodged the four final threats to Marty's (and Milt's and Bob's) well-being, Tom asked Bob if he really just saw what he thought he really just saw. "Were they who I thought they were?"

"They're look-alikes," said Bob.

"Including Campanella?"

"Absolutely."

"But he alluded to the famous visit we made to his house!" said Tom.

"That's 'cause I told him about it," said Bob, "on Welcome New Members Campfire Night."

"Why were they so pissed off?" asked Milt.

"Because," Bob said, "Marty wanted to free them—and his six other Sloyxneites—from the burden of their devotion to him by having them all drink poisoned Dr. Brown's cream soda."

"They coulda had Cel-Ray tonic," said Marty. "They had their choice of flavors, the sonsabitches, which none of Jim Jones's followers had, with his psychotic fuckin' 'raspberry only' rule."

Marty lamented that "the poison soda thing had worked pretty damn well for Jones in Guyana, and it would've worked well for M. Ron Sloyxne in Big Sur, too, if the sodas hadn't been rendered somehow suddenly poison-free. That's when what shall go down in religious history as the Sloyxne-gra-la Mutiny occurred."

"Why was the soda rendered suddenly poison-free?" asked Milt.

"Because," Marty said, rather embarrassed to have to admit it, "I didn't really wanna kill them. There was never really any poison in the soda, Mr. Stillasidioticasever! I was only trying to test their loyalty."

"You mean they got mad at you because you *didn't* really wanna kill 'em?"

"Yeah, and when they drank the shit and didn't die, they stopped thinking of me as their one true God or some crap. Lotsa sad people in this world, Milton, lots of very mixed-up, sad people."

"You mean to tell me," said Milt, "that the Willie Nelson and Tiger Woods and Julia Roberts and Roy Campanella look-alikes were willing to die for you?"

"Yessir," said Marty.

"Wow," said Milt. "Once a powerful man, always a powerful man."

Milt, ever hopeful but keeping his ever hope under wraps, asked his partner if he was through with religion now.

Marty said he thought that he was but would continue to be "only if Bob fulfills the promise he made to me." Tom looked in the rearview at Bob, who sent one of his patented Bob Sand eye rolls his way.

"What promise was that, Bob?" asked Tom.

"I promised him"—Bob could barely get the words out—"that if he'd shut down Sloyxne-gra-la and dissolve Silentexology, I'd help him deliver an audition tape he made to Robert Evans."

"Robert Evans the producer?"

"The kid stays in the picture!" shouted Marty, letting his little in-joke out into the car's interior before freeing another chilling "B-waaaah!" from its cage.

"What audition tape did you make without telling me?" Milt asked his partner.

"The one that's gonna get me the lead in *Godfather Three*. I'm a great actor now. I think I proved that in my historic role as M. Ron Sloyxne! And by the way, shutting down my religion wasn't the only promise I made to Mr. Big Head here," he said, referring to Bob. "You wanna tell 'em what else I promised you?"

"No," said Bob.

"I'll tell 'em, then," said Marty. "I also promised to go with Sand to see his old man, so's Mr. Big Head can ask the guy if he'll be his father in practice the way he was in a biological, life-giving context!"

"Your father?" Tom was amazed. Bob took a deep, frightened breath and nodded.

TEXAS DEATH CAGE MATCH

||||||||||||||||||||||||||

The marquee at the Olympic Auditorium, at the corner of 18th and Grand in downtown LA, let the world know that the main event of the evening would be an INDIAN DEATH MATCH: DR. JERRY GRAHAM VS. CHIEF CRAZY EAGLE!

Though Bob Sand's heart was racing, as he and Tom and Milt stared at the brightly lit marquee from their seats in Marty's hired limo as it approached the arena, it wasn't going anywhere near as fast as his mind. Bob hadn't seen his father in more than four years, nor spoken to him in more than two, and he had no idea how he might go about leaping across the wreckage of their personal history to ask him to be who he needed, more than anything, him to be. This was not, after all, *Father Knows Best*'s Jim Anderson with whom he'd be dealing; this was someone who'd been a self-absorbed physical culturist for sixty-two years, a man to whom there was nothing more important than making his muscles hard and his body beautiful, whose passion was the freedom of the road and whose sustenance was provided by the heat inherent in the arena, where, on a nightly basis, total strangers expressed their undying, unconditional love for the character he portrayed, which, over the course of thirty-nine years, had become more his true self than the disappointing true self the guy really was.

By the time the main event was about to begin Bob had almost forgiven Marty for his sins and was beginning to feel he might recover some of his life savings once the feds looked over the Sloyxne-gra-la books.

Marty tried desperately hard to get Bob allowed into his father's dressing room so that he could confront him face to face, but that failed because nobody believed that Bob was Crazy Eagle's child and because, as an LA cop who was there augmenting his income as a security goon for a so-called sport he detested said, "We get ten morons a week here who tell us that the Sheik or the Destroyer or Haystack Calhoun or Ricki Starr is their friggin' father!" Then, when all seemed lost—when Bob's father had already arrived in the ring, replete in his Native American full-feathered headdress, moccasins, beaded loincloth, and dyed black braided hair, and his bleached-blonde opponent, Dr. Jerry Graham, had begun his obnoxious strut down the aisle to the ring through a phalanx of hateful, bloodthirsty strangers—Marty grabbed Bob's hand, said "let's go!," and pulled Bob toward the ring at a gallop.

"What the hell are you doing, Marty?" shouted Bob as he and Marty raced down the aisle.

"If you want someone to be your father, kid, you gotta go to the source!" shouted Marty. "The source is down there, lookin' ridiculous under the hot lights, and you're gonna ask him now, you candy-assed son of a bitch, or never!"

Sloyxne squeezed Bob's hand as a cordon of security guards spotted them, clasped their own hands together, and formed a beefy human chain in front of the ring.

The height Marty achieved when he leaped—seven feet, easy, clearing the head of the tallest security goon by a good five inches—inspired the crowd, which also included Tom, to emit a collective gasp. And equally amazing was the fact that Bob leaped when Marty did and cleared that beefy human chain with inches to spare. When their bodies flew through the ropes and rolled in unison across the dirty canvas, the fans—ordinary blue-collar workers, for the most part, by day—erupted in a collective feral roar that was absolutely terrifying, even in his adrenalized state, for Bob to hear. The people knew, of course, that what was happening was for real. They knew it from the way Dr. Jerry Graham looked at Chief Crazy Eagle, and the way the two men let their ring personas fall away, for a fleeting moment, in order to defend themselves as a team against the two obvious "real" lunatics who'd had the balls and the madness to break the only rule—"Never ever touch the wrestlers"—in the otherwise fake world to which they (the fans) were, twice a week, granted limited entry. Even before Marty and Bob had gotten to their feet, Dr. Graham and Chief Crazy Eagle were all over them. Bob's father knocked Marty semiconscious with a right to the jaw and Graham punched Bob in the belly and was behind him before he fell, gasping for air, to his knees, a position from which Graham applied the sleeper hold (a real one), which would have put Bob to sleep and maybe even killed him had his father, Lou "Chief Crazy Eagle" Sand, not recognized him, at the last possible moment, and intervened.

Tom missed most of this, having fainted when the first salvo of perspiration swung out of the ring and onto his face.

"Hol' on, Jer," he said to Graham. "I think this idiot is my god-damned kid."

"Whoops," said the good doctor. "Apologies all around. Go, Lou, go."

"What the hell d'you think you're doing, Robbie?" asked Bob's father, as Dr. Graham strutted away so as to give his colleague, and his colleague's son, some much-needed time alone.

"I came here to ask you a question," said Bob, trying to ignore the fact that his father hadn't called him "Robbie" in a good ten years.

"This is my office you're in here," said the senior Sand. "This is where I do my work. Couldn't it have waited till later?"

"No," said his son.

"Then what the hell is it? What's your damned question?"

"Will you be my father?"

"Say *what*?"

"You heard me, Dad. Will you be my father or not?"

"Jesus Christ, kid," said Lou. "I answered that one when I walked out on you and your mother when you were ten, and the answer is the same now as it was then, which is 'No.' Fathering isn't for me, awright? I'm not good at that, I'm good at this, which is why I do this instead of that. Is that good enough for you?"

"Absolutely," said Bob.

"Good," said Lou. "Anything else?"

"Just one thing," said Bob.

He reached into his jacket, removed the old Polaroid photograph of him walking Brownie, handed it to his father, and said, "This is for you to keep."

Lou, who looked at the photo the way a man who's been caught looking at a photo of a dog he said never existed but whose existence has just been proven, looked up from the photo at Bob and said, "I got pissed off, awright? She crapped in the bathroom."

Before Bob could give him a final good-bye, Marty appeared with a folding chair raised over his head behind Dr. Graham, who whirled around just in time to grab the chair out of Marty's hand and whack Marty over his head with it, which knocked Marty flatter than a pancake and caused something that looked and felt and smelled very much like an actual riot to ensue, whose fires Bob then stoked by leaving the side of his biological father to go (to his own amazement) to the aid of Marty Sloyxne, who, although he wasn't Bob's real father, had put himself on the line for Bob in the way that real fathers do for their real sons. Bob picked up the folding chair Dr. Graham had dropped after flattening Marty with it, raised it over his head, ran toward Dr. Graham, and was hit over the head from behind with another folding chair wielded by Chief Crazy Eagle, who was, more than anything else— even more than he was Bob's father—a wrestler who lived by a certain code, the most important point of which was, "Protect your fellow worker, for he, more than anyone, puts bread on your table."

When Marty Sloyxne and Bob Sand woke up in adjoining beds the next morning at Cedars Sinai, their visitors, standing at the foot of their respective beds, were Milt Wagonman and Tom Leopold, who had just received a second tetanus shot for having been perspired on by professional wrestlers.

As Milt was embracing his newly awake partner as if he were a beloved mutt that had been lost for a year, Bob told Tom that he'd had the revelation, in the middle of the night—when a team of doctors had burst into the room and resuscitated Marty, who'd obviously died— that the thing for him to do was live his own life, one of the most important parts of which was to work once again with his dear friend Tom. "Bobby," Tom said, "that's music to my pants!"

Six weeks later to the day, Leopold and Sand would find out from CBS that their latest spec script, *Has Anyone Seen My Head?*, had gotten a green light for six episodes. The pilot, which starred the great dwarf actor Michael Dunn as the head, which sat atop the shoulders of a character named Melvin Checht, as played (from shoulders to feet) by Jamie Farr, would be the third show—including *Wright*, which was back on the air with a seminatural, flesh-toned Lucy Delle'bate, and the spin-off show, *You for Me and a Stew for You*—that Tom and Bob had running on the air. This fact was nowhere near as meaningful to the two men as just being back in the Biz, and back writing together again. Tom was so completely happy during the first few weeks that his nose bled continually.

TARZAN'S
TREE HOUSE

|||||||||||||||||||||||||||

Gwen had made good on her threat never to let Milt back in the house if he insisted on rescuing Marty, and Marty's landlord finally made good on his threat to "have his apartment condemned so that a biohazard team could get in and clean under his bed!"

Faced with the terrifying question of where they should go and what they should do next, Milt and Marty held in their hands a list of twenty-six available low-rent housing possibilities. Huddled together and sharing a single candied apple between them at a rainy-day table at an otherwise deserted Farmers Market, they chose to call the land-lord of a vacant Los Feliz district tree house. The tree house had been "hand-crafted, plank by plank" by famous movie Tarzan Johnny Weissmuller and was now being rented out by Weissmuller's twenty-nine-year-old son, Johnny Jr., who had begun overseeing the property as a way of augmenting his less than staggering income as the founder of Son of Tarzan Realty.

When Wagonman and Sloyxne arrived at the address, Marty was stunned to discover that what he remembered—from a Benzedrine orgy he'd attended, in 1956, at this very place—as a lush, magnificent estate had become overgrown with weeds, and that what had once been a breathtakingly beautiful antebellum-style mansion was now worn and peeling, and that the startlingly dramatic, once-pristine birch tree forest through which he remembered chasing a thick-legged nineteen-year-old starlet from Oklahoma, on that long-ago night, was now exploding with wild, unattended fauna. Before he had a chance to mourn the bygone splendor of the surroundings, Marty was grabbed around the wrist in a bone-crunching death grip by a huge, diapered chimpanzee that had appeared out of the blue and stuck an incredibly powerful paw through the iron gate and wouldn't let go, not even while it was yanking on its uncircum-sized little pink jungle schmeckie, the apparent ecstasy of which caused its wild brown eyes to ascend, balloonlike, into its Neanderthal skull. If Weissmuller Jr. had not shown up when he did, the terror Milt and Marty were feeling would most likely have stopped their hearts.

The barefoot, bare-chested, long-haired, loinclothed, pectorally gifted Johnny Weissmuller Jr. (who, by the way, was the spitting image of his father) soared across the horizon clinging to a green vine like some seminaked good-looking angel, in a prolonged arc high enough and dramatic enough to have been worthy of inclusion in any of his old man's old movies, before finally setting down in a precise pinpoint, landing atop the bony shoulders of the sexually aroused chimp, who started whirling on impact in a psychotic circle of rage and humiliation, thereby freeing Milt and Marty from its grasp. Tarzan's son rode the chimp's shoulders like a surfer before jumping off and shouting, "Cheeta Number Nine bad!," which sent the psychobeast and his fully engorged ape penis to scamper into the overgrown woods behind the house.

"Congratulations," said Weissmuller Jr., unlocking the gate from within.

"I beg your pardon?" replied Milt, rubbing his throbbing wrist.

"That was your interview, gentlemen, and you did good."

"That was it?"

"The only rule around here is that Cheeta Number Nine, who is a direct descendant of the original Cheeta in my dad's movies, has to love whoever lives on the property, and he clearly loves you guys a lot."

"So *that's* what love is," said Marty.

Milt and Marty cracked up alone.

"There's no joy in that laugh you're laughing, there, dudes," said the son of Tarzan.

"There's not?"

"And I know it. I feel the pain of others when I see it, dudes, and I feel your pain."

"That makes one of you," said Marty.

"I had the same pain, brother," said Johnny Jr., "the same nervous breakdown you two guys are obviously currently having, if you will."

"Nervous breakdown?" said Milt. "Oh, well, I don't think we're having—"

"Of course you don't, man. I was in denial for a long time, too, m'brother. Let me ask you this. Did you guys know your fathers?"

"Umm . . . I did know him. You would have liked him, wonderful man," replied Milt, lovingly.

"I wrote a very well received play about my dad," Marty said, topping his partner, "which was produced in New York."

"Good for you, dude. Do you know who *my* dad was? Johnny Weissmuller!"

"Are you sure that monkey liked us?" Milt wanted to know .

"He was Tarzan, man," said Weissmuller Jr. "My old man was Edgar Rice Burroughs's Tarzan, and he raised me to be my own person, live my own life, and develop my own style."

"Good for him and good for you," said Milt, making sure not to gawk at what he hoped was his and Marty's new landlord's long hair, leopard-skin loincloth, or the mile-long banana tree vine he'd swung in on.

Weissmuller Jr. whirled around like a game show model, swept his right arm across the expanse of the Declining Estate that Tarzan Built, and said, "The serenity of this place saved my life, man, and it'll do the same for you . . . if you let it."

No man dreams of spending the twilight of his years living in a pigeon shit–covered tree house that had been built by the late, great Johnny Tarzan Weissmuller. But as the at least equally great John Lennon said during one of the few moments he wasn't pretending to think Yoko was talented, "Life is what happens when you're busy making other plans," and for Milt and Marty other plans meant peeing into an empty Maxwell House coffee can, and eating fresh owl meat hanging off a nearby branch two hundred feet in the air, and collecting rain water in their Members Only jackets, and wringing it out into an impala horn . . . and, when they were not doing what they needed to do to stay alive, they were trying to write the "best damn let's get our asses back in the game" TV pilot spec in the history of television.

This time it was Milt who had the eureka moment. "I got it, Martin!"

"Not the runs again I hope!" Marty said over his shoulder, as he continued to lick sap from the tree root that held his hammock.

"Better than the runs," Milt said. "I just thought of a show idea so good it will get us out of this tree!" Milt's voice took on a Swedish schoolgirl's lilt of excitement as he waved his hands in the air and whirled about the tree house in a dervish victory jig.

"I'm listening, Milton." Marty had no faith in the coming idea but "what the fuck," he thought, it beat looking out the window at that dead squirrel's petrified ass.

"And it shall be called *A Bridge for Raymond*!" Milt held for a beat for Marty to drink in the title. When Marty was done drinking, Milt continued. "I thought, for good luck, we'd use your son Ray's name in the title. Think about it, Martin! In all our years, we've never once wrote a show with a kid as the lead."

Marty interrupted Milt's roll to remind him that in 1965 they had written *A New Tony for the Mitchell Family*, about a family called the Mitchells who lived in a town called Spring Place who, each episode, adopted a different boy named Tony after their biological son, Anthony Jr., ran off with an older man he'd met on a streetcar after the refined man had compared their son to a "Greek god."

"This is nothing like *A New Tony*, Martin . . . and even if it was, nobody'll remember that show, 'cause we lost our only copy of it when you threw it at that fishing boat in San Pedro harbor."

"Oh, right," Marty said, recalling the incident. "So we're good. Okay, Milton, give! This *A Bridge for Raymond* of yours, where do you see it going? Where's the franchise?"

"Here's the franchise, my friend," Milt spritzed on, even though the ideas were coming faster than he could breathe bad denture breath into them. "It'll be about a kid who dreams of having his own bridge someday!" With that, Milt stopped talking and waited, as sure of his invention as Edison must have been about the phonograph for Marty to leap off the broken apple box they used for a chair and embrace him.

"That's it?" Marty asked, leaping off of nothing and embracing nobody.

Milt nodded fiercely, still positive he had hit the mother lode. Marty told his partner that he would have preferred Milt's still having the runs to a show called *A Bridge for Raymond*. Milt wrote off the lack of enthusiasm to Marty's being old and broke, despised by everyone, and living like an ape in a dying tree, and forced his pal to at least write some dialogue along with him for the spec. "Come on, Marty. You know how you are when you turn on the ol' dialogue tap."

They had no paper so Milt took off his T-shirt and transcribed Marty's spitballed dialogue across the garment with the ballpoint pen, chain still attached, that he had borrowed from the bank.

"Okay, I'll try," Marty said. "But I don't promise anything!" Milt told Marty that he couldn't pitch bad dialogue if his life depended on it. Marty smiled in agreement and fell right into character as Raymond.

RAYMOND: Dad, how's about you getting me a bridge?

RAYMOND'S DAD: A bridge, Raymond? Why in great Caesar's ghost would you need a bridge, son? Why Ray, we live not within twelve hundred miles of a body of water!

RAYMOND: I need that bridge, Dad. It's my dream.

"Slow down, Martin," Milt shouted, putting stolen pen to soiled shirt, afraid of missing a word.

RAYMOND'S DAD (slower): I had a dream once too, young Ray boy. I forgot what it is now, but if it's a bridge you'll be a-wantin', it's a bridge you'll be a-gettin'. As God is my copilot, son, you'll get you your bridge! And it'll be an expansion bridge, too, with a toll booth with a disgruntled employee in it and a path where lovers can walk off a heavy meal.

Nothing beats a good day's work to help one, or in this case two, to forget one's troubles. And before either wordsmith knew it, the moon had risen above the gaping hole of their roof and sleep beckoned to the two men, who were comforted in the knowledge that they could once again storm the Bastille of show business, armed now with an entire T-shirt of ideas. This fact only made it harder for Milt to understand why Marty, after drinking a whole bottle of absinthe, disappeared into the hills after carving these words into the tree house floor: "I thought *I* was the idea guy and *you* were the structure guy? How dare you yousurp [*sic*] my place in the partnership! P.S. I banged your wife, during which time she screamed out, Split me in half, Daddy

Milt & Marty

Longlegs, with your big blue Seabiscuit cock! This, by the way, she said in Yiddish. Best personal regards. M.S. P.P.S. I went to heed the coyote's call, so don't look for me! P.P.P.S. Go fuck yourself! P.P.P.P.S. It also depressed me a little to live in a tree house."

Milt just couldn't get his mind around Marty's abandoning him and their new project *and* sleeping with his wife, in that order! Everything had finally started to go their way. They had a bright, fully worked out show to pitch, and there was still half a guava left for breakfast and no raccoons had climbed into the tree house to bite at their faces.

"I don't think I will ever understand Martin Sloyxne!" a shattered Milt remarked to Carl, the dead squirrel he and Marty had come to think of as their own. "What could a coyote give him that I could not?"

Milt was dealt another blow, on the day after Marty had run high into the Hollywood Hills, when Johnny Weissmuller Jr., the son of Johnny Weissmuller Sr. and a man whom Milt had always felt always liked Marty best, appeared at the base of the tree house wearing nothing but the trail diaper his father had worn in the film *White Bwana Woman and the Devil Jewel* and told Milt that he was giving him forty-eight hours' notice before he would have to move out of the tree house so that he could move in.

"I'm sorry, Mr. Wagonmaster," he said, making the same mistake he'd made with Milt's name since he and Marty first moved in. "But financial realities have forced me to rent out the big house, and the Dutch rock band that wants it needs to move in on Thursday." With a heavy heart, Milt bid good-bye to the lopsided, rotting, army ant–infested tree house he and Marty had called home and shimmied down the rope ladder for the last time . . . but not before carving the words "*A Bridge for Raymond* was conceived here" onto the tree house floor.

KING O'
THE GYPSIES

||||||||||||||||||||||||||

Milt never came right out and asked his wife to take him back. He simply laid down under the back wheels of Gwen's car and hollered for his wife to "come outside and run me over! Just crush my pelvis, darling, 'cause that's all I deserve after what I've put you through!" Gwen, still smarting from Milt's leaving and for his forsaking Judaism for the Marty religion, took Milt's dare all the way up to the point of switching on the ignition before bursting into tears, switching off the engine, and running back behind the car to embrace her beloved Milt, only to find him already inside the house making himself a plate of salami and eggs.

The life that Milt built with Gwen in the months following the end of what Milt called "my Marty period" had its pluses. For one thing, the five hours of sleep he started getting each night were twice as many as he'd averaged during the course of his fifty-six-year partnership with "the Coyote Man of the Hollywood Hills," as Gwen referred, rather unfairly Milt thought, to his missing partner. Another bright spot for Milt was the "perfect Presbyterian weather" they were having that spring, and how it began to lift "the black tarpaulin of depression from the infield of his personality," as a longtime neighbor, a retired

183

major league baseball players' union psychologist, had explained to him, causing Milt to be reasonably content for at least five days out of every seven, which, according to the retired narcoleptic rabbi who lived three doors down from him and Gwen, "may be the highest ratio ever achieved by a Jew in the history of mankind."

Yet for all of these "half pluses," as Milt himself referred to the pleasures of his life, there was one overwhelming minus: Milt missed show business. He ached for all of it, especially the camaraderie. And regardless of how much fun taking advantage of the many recreational activities Gwen so lovingly forced down his throat—golf, bowling, squeezing and discarding grapefruit at market—Milt just couldn't find the same delicious well of contentment and sense of creative abandon that had made him feel so stunningly alive in the godawfully profane, irreverent atmosphere of even the worst comedy writing room.

Somewhere in the middle of his twenty-sixth week away from the Business, therefore, Milt began the zombification process otherwise known as "compulsive regular weekday television viewing." Starting with *The Today Show* each day, he would stare at the screen hoping against hope that Ann Curry would just once, "one lousy stinkin' time, for godsakes!," uncross those fabulous waxed goyish half-Asian legs of hers so that he might get a peek at her thousand-dollar panties, and he wouldn't move his ass off the cushion, except to visit the bathroom, or eat the salmon spread lunch Gwen made for him each day before she left for her Tai-Chi in a Chair class and her Ladies' Meaningful Conversation (Speak Only If You Want To) Group Luncheon Followed by Tea.

Milt noticed that his wife was becoming, thanks to her expensive new improvement classes, the girl full of life whom she'd started out in life to be. He, by contrast, began only to enjoy using the word "shit" over and over again. It became as much a part of his daily repartee with Gwen as the deep sighs that each exasperated spouse regularly expelled. "Where the shit is my shittin' knockoff Rolex, Gwen?" he'd want to know, and "What the shit is this green leafy shit next to my chicken tenders, Gwen?"

Gwen, who'd never before heard the man utter one foul word, became so concerned about him that she insisted he go talk to a professional once again. Perhaps since Dr. Pearl Kubler-Roth, their last therapist, had been a woman, this was the reason he didn't benefit from the sessions as much as she. "You need a man doctor, darling," Gwen offered lovingly, "someone with a similar background and genitals to you."

The similar-genitaled person Gwen found for her husband was their major league baseball players' union psychologist friend, Marv Pumistone. After some coaxing, Milt agreed to meet at a municipal golf course coffee shop, where Milt almost instantaneously revealed that he no longer trusted his wife.

"When did the trust start to erode?" asked Dr. Pumistone, while ordering an Arnold Palmer.

"Within an hour of hearing on good authority that she'd had sex with my former partner. What's an Arnold Palmer?"

"Lemonade and iced tea. Who's the good authority?"

"My former partner. I'll have an Arnold Palmer too," Milt told the waiter.

"Your former partner told you that?"

"Yes."

"And you believed him?"

"Absolutely."

"Was he someone whose word was usually gold?"

"No, his word was usually shit. A big tube of shit paste squeezed out on a shit toothbrush."

"Then why did you believe him?"

"Because," said Milt, "he described something Gwen did that only a person who was participating in the act of schtupping the shit out of her could've known."

"Which was what?"

"Which was a certain something she said in Yiddish."

"What did she say?"

" 'Split me in half, Daddy Longlegs, with your big blue Seabiscuit cock!' "

Dr. Pumistone's reaction—the way the blood drained from his face and his cheek muscles made an involuntary quiver—told Milt that the good doctor himself had also banged Gwen.

"You schtupped her, too, didn't you, Mr. Shit-for-brains?" asked the recently assertive and paranoid Wagonman.

After his therapy lunch, the only true breakthrough of which turned out to be Milt's falling in love with lemonade and iced tea mixed together, Milt became more and more withdrawn. He could barely get out of bed in the morning and he soon stopped talking altogether. Nothing pierced his silence, not even when Gwen burst into tears and said, "Would you at least say the word 'shit' again, for goodness sake?"

Later that very same day, after her second Advanced Yoga with No Fruit at the Bottom Thursday class, Gwen Wagonman left her husband.

"You live your life and I'll live mine. It's official, sweetie, I'm letting go of you, and from this moment on you're free. My hope in doing this is that you will find Milt Wagonman as I have found Gwendolyn Zanitz, and that somewhere along the way our separate roads might converge and you and I might reconnect."

Too stunned by this news to remember his own wife's maiden name, Milt weakly asked who Gwendolyn Zanitz was, and "Why is any of *our* business suddenly *her* business?"

Milt & Marty

Milt was fast asleep on a certain Tuesday afternoon, a few days after Gwen had let go of him, when his doorbell rang.

"Shit!" said Milt, before pulling his bedsheet up over his eyes. The doorbell kept ringing. "Who the shit can that be," he wondered, "on a shitty Tues-shit-day afternoon?"

The bell ringing, which continued for a good three minutes, was followed by violent pounding on the door.

"What the shitcube!" said Milt out loud, before kicking off his sheet, throwing on his robe, and making his furious way down the carpeted stairway leading to the living room he now shared with no one.

When he opened the door he couldn't believe his eyes. A crazy-eyed, rotund Gypsy, with a full red beard and matching unkempt forest of bandanna'd hair, stood there in the flamboyant red and yellow silks of, as Milt surmised, his particular amoral sect. His black eyes were blazing and his beefy arms were folded across his defiantly puffed-out chest as he asked, in severely wounded English, "Eetz dots you cah, meeshtawr?"

"I beg your pardon?" asked Milt.

"Dee Foul-cone! Dee Foul-cone!" shouted the Gypsy, pointing toward the driveway at Milt's car. "Eetz dots you cah, dee Foul-cone, oh nut?"

On the previous occasions in his life when the frustrations of hard-to-understand foreigners had frightened him, Milt had always been able to call upon his amazing ability to decipher whatever garbled thing it was that said frightening individual was saying. All he needed, usually, was a third chance.

"Could you say that one more time, please?" asked Milt.

"Dee fockin Fort Foul-cone!" shouted the exasperated Gypsy. "Eetz dee fockink Fort Foul-cone yooz cah, oh nut?"

"Yessir," said Milt, calmly. "The fucking Ford Falcon is my car."

"Hukkeh, den!" said the Gypsy. "Ha boud hi feex hall dee dinks hahn det sombeets Fort Foul-cone fah tvenna fie dolliz?"

"Do you really mean all the dings on that son-of-a-bitch Falcon?" asked Milt. "You'll fix all the dings on it for just twenty-five dollars?"

"Ya!" said the Gypsy. "Hall ah dem! Hall dem fockink dinks hon det cogsogeenk pizza sheet fah chust tvenna fie box!"

"What if I have no cash?"

"Yah kin peh mih weed ah sheck, den!"

"I guess we have a deal, then," said Milt.

"Goot!" said the Gypsy, who then extended his beefy right hand and asked, "Moy nem ees King JoJo, and hi yam dee kink huff hall dee Chipseez!"

"Nice to meet you, King JoJo, the king of all the Gypsies," said Milt. "My name is Wagonman and I am the king of nothing."

It felt good to Milt, as he sat on his front step and watched the Gypsy attempt to remove the multitude of dings from his Falcon, that the flamboyant stranger hadn't killed him, which, in the light of his long-standing dark attitude toward life, surprised him. Maybe what I really want, he thought to himself, is to live. Just then, as if cued by some invisible director in a heartwarming movie, the Gypsy looked up at Milt from his ding removal work and said, "Gas wad, meeshtawr?"

"What?"

"Teck ha gas."

"I've never been good at guessing," said Milt. "Please just tell me."

"Hukkeh. Hi chust deed ha lod muh den tvenna fie dolliz woita woik on yuh cah."

"Whaddya mean, you just did a lot more than twenty-five dollars worth of work on my car?"

"You vahn hi shoot rahpeetz eat?"

"No, I want you should stick to your word."

"Vords har like dih hushin, meeshtawr . . . day chendj veet d'ecktivity hoff dah moon."

"'They change with the activity of the moon,' my doggoned derriere," said Milt. "You quoted me a price of twenty-five dollars, goddammit, and I'm not gonna pay you one penny more than that, and that's—"

Before Milt could say "final," the Gypsy had reached down into the area where just his underpants and genitalia should have been and pulled out a long dagger, the point of which he pressed against the delicate flesh of Milt's involuntarily quivering left eyelid as he said, "Hi deet tree time de vork hi yootchally dewey fur tvenna fie dolliz, meeshtawr, vitch minz yah ho mee juan huntreet dolliz."

"Why would I owe you one hundred dollars?" asked Milt. "Three times twenty-five is seventy-five."

"Beecuts yah peesed mih hoff tvenna fie hextra dolliz voit!" said the Gypsy.

"Wait here, then," said Milt, "while I go inside and get a check."

"Hi dun hicksept shecks," said the Gypsy. "Kesh hunly."

"But you said you would take a check!"

"Hi yam ah potholeogical lieyar, meeshtawr. Vie you tink my peoples makes me derr king?"

Gwen nearly fainted when Milt's Falcon, which Milt was driving with the Gypsy king as his passenger to the bank to withdraw a C-note from Milt and Gwen's savings, passed her. Having just left her Friday morning Kagelomics: Strengthening Your Vagina Muscle While Making It More Efficient class, she was feeling enough compassion for Milt to forgive him, which she looked forward to doing in person. But then, when she saw the Falcon and focused her eyes on Milt, who was behind the wheel in his robe and pajamas next to the crazy-looking Gypsy who was waving and wiggling his lascivious tongue at her as they passed, she decided instead to buy herself a "grudge latte" at the nearest Starbucks.

The ride back from the bank was a low point—maybe the lowest point ever—in Milt's life. As the Gypsy king sat counting Milt's freshly withdrawn cash in the passenger seat, Milt thought about putting his right foot to the Falcon's flimsy floor and crashing into the rear of the potato chip delivery truck that was stopped at a red light in front of them. Staring at the four huge letters painted across the eighteen-wheeler's gleaming rear panels, Milt thought, If there's one damned thing I haven't been in this poop of a life it's "wise." He thought of the irony and couldn't help but smile. Gwen would get a big kick out of it, he decided, every time she told her enlightened new friends that the closest her dope of a dead husband had ever gotten to wise was when he suicided his car into a truck that had that word emblazoned on its surface.

By the time the light had changed, though, Milt's suicidal impulse had passed, and he was pondering the maddening Wagonmanian predictability of such a wasted opportunity when the Gypsy king said, "A painy foor yah taughts, Meeshtawr Vogginmahn."

"I have no thoughts," said the deeply depressed Milt. "Only wise men have thoughts, and if I had one it wouldn't even be worth a penny. By the way, how do you know my name?"

"Why you morose, self-pitying prick, you!" said JoJo the Gypsy king, whose accent was suddenly devoid of anything resembling Gypsy but reeked Brooklyn and the Bronx and a few of the more deprived neighborhoods of Jersey City. "You should be ashamed of yourself!" Trying, and failing, to comprehend what was going on, Milt blinked, which inspired the Gypsy king to sing: "Ever know another like me, pal? An escapee so full of bold glee? Out of Quentin all the way to D.C., pal? Another like Bobby B. Free?"

Milt knew those words because he and Marty had written them as the theme song for an escaped convict pilot of theirs called *B. Free on the Run.*

Milt & Marty

Milt was struck as if by lightning by the realization that the Gypsy king wasn't a Gypsy king at all but his crazy, brilliant chameleon of an ex-partner, the death-defying Marty Sloyxne himself, who then put one of his fat hands around the back of Milt's head, gently grasped his neck, and said, "Why are you so fuckin' depressed, my beloved Milty? If it's 'cause you think I fucked your wife you can relax, because I didn't."

When Milt's feral sobbing subsided, he was able to look Marty in the eyes and whisper, "You didn't?"

"Of course I didn't, you pathetic geriatric pile of schmuck meat!"

"Then how did you know about the 'Split me in half, Daddy Long-legs, with your big blue Seabiscuit cock!' in Yiddish thing?"

"Because you told me about it yourself, you oblivious little putz!"

"I told you about it?"

"During one of the ten thousand fuckin' naps you took when we were doin' our *Seven Is a Five-Letter Word* pilot, you asshole!"

"Oh my God," said a stunned Milt. "Of course! During the time we were doing *Seven*, I was being treated by Dr. Peter J. Nazzarmenth at the Beverly Hills Sleep Disorder Institute for talking in my sleep!'"

"Exactly, my dick," said Marty. "And not to change the subject or anything, but how come every fuckin' thing you say sounds like a fuckin' late-night infomercial?"

Before Milt and Marty were halfway back to Milt's house, Milt had asked Marty to stay with him "at least until you get back on your feet."

"What the hell does back on my feet mean?" asked a too easily offended Marty.

"You know," said Milt. "Just till the psychosis passes and you no longer believe you're the king of the fuckin' Gypsies."

Marty sat Milt down and straightened him out about his conversion to Gypsianism. How it wasn't a psychosis at all but "the only true way to live, that is, if you can't be in show business," and how Marty came to be crowned king. It happened soon after he'd answered the "proud coyote's call" and after only a few minutes of hanging out with "that idiot coyote," Marty climbed down out of the hills to get a cold beer at T.G.I.F.'s, which is where he met, and ended up courting, on that night, a four-hundred-pound Gypsy woman who, although she'd been born Miriam Lefkowitz, had since 1953 been going by the name Fire Dancer and was accepted by the natural-born members of her Gypsy band as one of them. Fire Dancer was not merely the Gypsy queen and Marty Sloyxne's tenth wife; she was also his Gypsy mentor, who taught him the ropes regarding the fine art of the scam, hundreds of which she knew like no one else, and one of which—the Ripping Off Old People by Promising to Replace Their Roof for Six Hundred Dollars and Then Skipping Town with Their Money con—became Marty's raison d'être, his specialty, the reason, he came to think, that he'd been put on this earth. Although Fire Dancer was married (according to Gypsy law) to Marty, her true love was Prince Renaldo, the driver of the Gypsy bus and the only man in America (or so he said) "who makes Milton Berle look like a girl, if you catch my drift," which Fire Dancer caught on a nightly basis while Marty was passed out in his and Fire Dancer's love tent from the red homemade Gypsy table wine.

For whatever reason, Marty and the Gypsy life clicked. After Fire Dancer died of a ruptured appendix at the annual Gypsy Enclave, held only days before all of this on a Rent It By the Night Week or Month onion field near Bakersfield, California, Marty, who had just eaten an entire roast goat and imbibed the equivalent of a case of red wine from a pig bladder in his departed wife's honor, broke into a whirling, feverish, highly emotional, overtly sexual mourning dance, which so moved and excited the other Gypsies that they placed a handmade

Post-It Crown of I.O.U.s on his head, after which he was named "King of the Gypsies" by all twenty-five members of his new flock, which broke up into twelve impulsive sexual couplings, right there on the dirty, radioactive earth before the stunned eyes of their new king—who, because the only other single besides him was Prince Renaldo, opted, as he put it, "to—what the hell—learn something new. I mean, if Grace Kelly could get banged by a prince . . ."

After exhaling through his nose like a spent bison, Marty gave Milt a long hard look and asked, "Now sir, after hearing that, do you still believe my being a Gypsy is a psychosis? What *is* a psychosis, anyway?" Before Milt could define the word, a half dozen police and FBI vehicles parked right outside the Wagonman home, which was a good thing since Milt really wasn't all that sure how to define "psychosis."

The police and the FBI, to say nothing of Gwen Wagonman, were so stymied by Milt's refusal to press extortion and kidnapping charges against Marty that they all stomped off—the cops and the feds to their respective beats and Gwen to the master bedroom to pack what she hadn't already packed of her belongings, never to look back on her way to a condo co-owned by Rusti Boxe and Jo Van Heflin, two retired whitewater-rafting guides from Washington State whom Gwen had met at a Sunday evening slide show about time-share rentals in Maine. Milt's reaction upon watching Gwen stomp out of the house with a huge suitcase in either hand was to look at Marty and say something he knew not to be true in his heart but that he knew Marty would enjoy hearing: "I was more married t' you, ya crazy bastard, than I ever was t' her!"

Five minutes later, Milt sat in a folding beach chair—a spectator in his own bathroom, as mesmerized as a ten-year-old watching his father shave—as Marty took an elaborate Gypsy bath in a tubful of water that had been beautified by the "multitudinous colorful cleansing crystals mined by my very own Gypsy peoples from the core guts of the rich and luscious New Mexican crimson Devil's clay, the texture of which is as close to my mama's sponge cake as anything I have ever seen on this rotating scab the so-called scientists call earth!"

As Marty explained it to Milt, the "Gypsy Bath Song," which lies at the very heart of the ritual—or *ritua*, as Marty called it—must always be sung "at full voice, whilst the singer's testicles are cupped in the hand nearest Milwaukee, Wisconsin. Why Milwaukee? Experts believe that it has something to do with the word 'Milwaukee' itself, which bares a striking resemblance to the word 'Millwokee,' which is Gypsy slang for millworker, each of whom have, historically speaking, been a favorite mark or target for the Milwonka, which is a Gypsy Ponzi scheme, whereby one millworker is told by the worker next to him, a secret Gypsy informer, that his foreman is trying to kill him and that he can save himself only by coercing two of his best friends to chloroform the foreman and drive him to Milwaukee, Wisconsin, on the fender of his car, at which time three previously kidnapped millworkers will at once be driven back by the milworpna, or transport Gypsy—usually a hermit with absolute or near perfect pitch—to a small end table mill in Milwaukee, Pennsylvania, population sixty-two."

Though the words to the "Gypsy Bath Song" vary from tribe to tribe, their commonality rests in the fact that they all center around the themes of cleanliness and petty larceny: "Scrub so the suckers come up with the cash / Scrub, scrub, scrub till there's a shine on you a(h)ss / If you scrub like the Jews took over the banks / Gypsy keep the dough and the world can keep its 'thanks!' / Scrub, scrub, dubba, dub, deedle, de bunny / I wish I had all d' honest folk money / Wash wash wash but don't y' wash off your cod / I wish I di'n have t' work so ha(h)d / and I wish I could break this endless cycle / of low-level crime and pointless nomadic traveling . . ."

Milt & Marty

In the middle of Marty/King JoJo's song, Milt burst into tears. Marty was concerned but played the tough love card—"What the fuck are you blabberin' about, you pathetic wifeless, assless old heeb?"

Gathering his inner forces to the extent that he possessed any, Milt told his ex–comedy writing partner turned dashing Gypsy sovereign that he, Marty, had become "the most magnificent creature I have ever laid eyes on," and then he went even further. "I feel blessed and graced and gifted, and it's a mitzvah to think that I, Milton Abraham Lincoln Wagonman, an inappropriately middle-named nobody from Brooklyn, New York, once had the privilege of writing hundreds of unproduced sitcom pilots with a great man like you!" Milt took a deep breath and got to his secondary point, his first point having been nothing more than a compliment, really. "And, King JoJo, I speak to you from an honest heart when I say that I would very much like to join your band of merry Gypsies . . . if, that is, you happen to have an opening at the present time."

The poignant, all-naked induction-baptism ceremony in Milt's bathtub was followed by an adornment ceremony wherein Milt was presented with a complete Gypsy wardrobe, while the significance of each sacramental garment was explained to him and blessed by King (Marty) JoJo, utilizing the spitting of ginger ale onto the back of Milt's head by said king (who, near the end of the ceremony, slipped in the tub and cracked his dental plate in half, while grabbing for the unflushed toilet).

The Traditional Gypsy Adornment Ceremony Clothes

1. The Scrog, or Gypsy headpiece, fashioned from the old honeymoon douche bag Gwen Wagonman had most recently used to hide travelers checks in. To secure the scrog at the correct rakish angle on Milt's head, the douching hose had to be wound twice around Milt's chin and

the nozzle lowered down his back, cinched, and anchored to the rusty metal clasp of the truss he'd been wearing since his disastrous 1956 double hernia operation.

2. The Django Reinhardt, or "red blouse of the lark," slang endemic to Marty's tribe; Lark is a newly inducted Gypsy. The rules for this require that the Gypsy king "run naked and wet from inside the nest of the Lark" down to "the nearest curb" in order to cut "a swatch of upholstery from the nearest available automobile belonging to someone else"—in this case, from the seat of a 1971 Cadillac convertible, which had once been owned by Vidiligo Jones, a Hollywood pimp who'd somehow been befriended by the Caddy's current owner, retired pharmacist Sol Electrowitz, a neighbor of Milt's. After breaking into Dr. Electrowitz's Caddy and liberating the upholstery swatch—the entire seat cover, actually—from its backseat, Marty cut two arm holes through it and slipped it over Milt's head without upsetting his scrog, during which the outraged Dr. Electrowitz, who had just discovered that his Caddy had been vilified, stood in his white terry-cloth robe and said into his cell phone, in a louder voice than he'd called upon in years, "I want the members of your department to respond to my plight as quickly as possible, officer! My car has been stolen and that is not acceptable!"

3. The Kojak, or waist sash, which must be wrapped eleven times around the Lark, represents the first eleven character actors ever to play a Gypsy in a movie, television show, or discount appliance store opening. For Milt's Kojak, King JoJo poured a bottle of mercurochrome over the shower curtain, stiffened it with leftover chicken fat, and then "Gypsy stitched" it inside a throw rug. King JoJo then commanded his Lark to rotate in a semiclockwise manner until both men became so dizzy they had to lie down for the rest of the day.

Milt & Marty

After they awoke and drank a cup of Postum, King JoJo/Marty offered Milt a new Gypsy name, Willie Princebone, given by his king to acknowledge the "regal aloofness" of Milt's penis, which Marty had never theretofore seen.

The bliss felt by both comedy writers at becoming joined now in the Gypsy blood was suddenly shattered by a call to King JoJo's stolen Gypsy cell phone from the Philippines, where Marty's second wife, Marilyn Catotocan Sloyxne de Benevides de la Guerra, was calling to tell her ex that she'd just received an emergency call from the California mental facility where their fifty-one-year-old son, Raymond, had spent a good two-thirds of his life. And then Marty heard the words every father dreads. A fellow patient up at Raymond Sloyxne's mental facility dropped a huge dollhouse on Ray-Ray's head after Ray-Ray had locked all the patients in the dayroom and forced them to watch a *Wizard of Oz* video two thousand times—enraging one patient with multiple personalities to such a degree he clobbered Ray-Ray with the metal dollhouse once for each of his six personalities. Fortunately, for Marty's son, one of the nutjob's personalities happens to be the late, elderly poetess Marianne Moore, so "he didn't hit Raymond so hard that time." Still, the tragic fact remained that Raymond Errol Flynn Sloyxne, Marty's only child and heir, now lay in a deep coma.

Marty loosened his scrog at the terrible news, and then he asked his ex-wife what she planned to do about the situation. Marty was from the old school and believed a son's coma was the mother's obligation.

Marilyn, never known as a "count on her when the chips are down" person, responded to Marty's query with, "How the fuck should I know what to do about it, you old pussy-bewitched bastard?"

"I don't know, you sagging, penis-allergic bitch, you," offered Marty in reply, still trying to keep his voice at an even keel, "but what the fuck do you want me to do about it?"

"I have no idea, you sphincter of a farmer's syphilitic weekend fuck pig. But you'd better go up there and get him out of that coma before they toss Ray-Ray out of that hospital. They don't want coma people up there. It makes it hard for them to get funding."

Marty asked why, even though Marilyn and he had never gotten along, she couldn't find it within her heart to join him at the institution, "because even though he hates your guts, the presence of his mother might help revive our beloved boy."

"Because," Benevides de la Guerra replied, "I'm half a world away in the country of Chad doing makeup and hair for the Miss Third World competition, that's why! You handle something for once in your pathetic life, powder cum!"

"Rhino douche!" Marty screamed into the cell phone just before throwing it through the large bay window of the Wagonmans' living room.

As quickly as Marty had become enraged, though, he experienced the kind of instant calm a sane person might, and then it hit him. "I know how to do it," he said to himself, loud enough for Milt to hear.

"You know how to do *what*?" asked Milt, who had run into the room at the sound of all the shattering glass.

"How to get my Ray-Ray to come out of his schizophrenically induced coma," Marty proclaimed, as he turned to face his Gypsy second in command.

"Ray-Ray's in a coma? No wonder you broke the only nice window in this house." Milt, who could still remember holding Ray-Ray's twenty-eight-pound body in his arms within hours of the boy's birth, was saddened by the emotional hit his king had suffered.

"It makes perfect sense!" said Marty.

"What, breaking my window?" asked Milt.

"No, ass breath! Why my boy would force a bunch of mental

defectives to watch *The Wizard of Oz* two thousand times before they turned on him. You remember how much my little boy always loved that schmaltzy picture?"

"Sure I do," said Milt. "The poor kid was obsessed with that feel good musical!"

"Right," said Marty. "So he probably wanted that nutcase to drop the dollhouse on his head as a way for Raymond to finally make his way *into* the film itself."

"You should be a psychiatrist, Marty."

"Would you shut up, Milt? I've got a son in a coma here and you're sitting here kissing my ass!"

Milt apologized for the compliment.

"Apology accepted. Come on!" King JoJo commanded.

"Where to, my king?"

Marty removed from his dewsnap, or Gypsy wallet, a folded newspaper story he'd torn from the *Lompoc Times* while he and his Gypsy band were scamming the elderly citizens near there. The story concerned Walter Kliebt, one of the oldest living (at ninety-eight) Munchkins, who, on that day, happened to be about to embark on a tour of West Coast junior high schools and universities where he would speak to students not only about his performance in *The Wizard of Oz* but about the challenges imposed by his midgetism and how he overcame them.

"He's here," said Marty.

"Who's here?" asked Milt.

"The Munchkin."

"Here in the house? Did he break my window?"

"No numbnuts. In California, on his speaking tour. So here's what we're gonna do next . . ."

" 'We,' king of all Gypsydom?" asked Milt.

"Unless, of course, you don't wanna help me," said Marty.

"Surely, my liege jokes!" said Milt, bowing slightly.

"A Gypsy thank you, kid. And by the way, it thrills me no end that you're finally using curse words. It's about fuckin' time, man. We're goin' to West LA, brother."

"Why the fuck-prick are we gonna do that?"

"Because," said Marty, pointing at the Walter Kliebt article. "This little Munchkin guy—and this is the God's little miracle part right here—happens to be the only living creature on earth who can save my poor Ray-Ray. He's scheduled to be just a few fuckin' miles away today talkin' at a school about what it was like to be in *The Wizard of* fuckin' *Oz* and, well, I'll tell you, Milton, this set of circumstances was heaven fuckin' sent and God fuckin' made for us, my Gypsy brother, and if you and me grab little Mr. Kliebt and tuck him under our arm and run with him like he's a football down to Ray-Ray's nuthouse in Gardena and wave him over my unconscious boy, well, I believe my son will wake up!"

Milt was stunned by the inspired simplicity of the plan. "No wonder they elected you king."

Willie Princebone curtsied in awe. Marty told him to "save the homo stuff and fire up the Falcon." Milt asked permission to put a plastic sheet over the broken bay window but Marty nixed it, saying there just wasn't time. Marty also lied about seeing a weather report predicting no rain that day and, truth be told, it did not rain, but a burglar did enter the Wagonman home through the busted window, stealing Milt's televisions, the watch his father had given him at his bar mitzvah, a brand-new set of bath towels, and half a dozen pairs of Gwen's (high-waisted) underpants.

WITH A MUNCHKIN
IN MY PANTS

||||||||||||||||||||||||||||||

Milt and Marty drove like the devil to Emerson Junior High School in West LA, where the Munchkin Walter Kliebt was to give his standard $250-a-pop motivational lecture, "It's Okeydoke to Be Different!," to a group of seventh, eighth, and ninth graders gathered in the auditorium.

Wagonman and Sloyxne, the king and his court, entered and stood as inconspicuously as possible, given their Gypsy outfits, at the back of the packed venue in close proximity to Claire Yamanaguchi, a Japanese-American ABC *Eyewitness News* reporter, who was there to cover the Munchkin's speech. Ms. Yamanaguchi, who like most ethnic TV journalists was normally relegated to weekend TV anchor duties, had been given this plum assignment totally on her merits. Ms. Yamanaguchi approached Milt and Marty and inquired about the "colorful clothing, shower curtain, throw rug, and douche bag" they were wearing. Marty explained that they were old friends of Walt's and that they too had appeared in the classic *Wizard of Oz* in "the never-seen big Gypsy musical number, which depicted Auntie Em agreeing to have her roof fixed by Gypsies, only to have them cash her check and skip town without doing the work—"

"—moments before the twister hit and blew her roof off anyway," Milt added, trying to round out the story.

"Which is why, Ms. Yamanaguchi," said Marty, "Willie Princebone here and I are now glad that our scene, which was filmed in our pre-Gypsy enlightenment days, was cut from the movie. As we would now, in our elevated Gypsy states of mind, be deeply troubled by our participation in something so negative toward our beloved peoples."

For the next forty minutes, Milt and Marty regaled the reporter with many fondly remembered lies about having been part of the "onset magic" that was "rampant" during the filming of *The Wizard of Oz*. When Walter Kliebt had completed his speech (the last line of which was "From one midget to a bunch of others, kids . . . stay off the drugs!"), the auditorium exploded in cheers from children so elated by the fact that the scary little man had finally stopped talking they rushed the stage and engulfed him in a chaotic swarm of pimply hysteria. Among the hordes rolling and shifting like one giant "we'll do anything not to return to the classroom" organism were Milt and Marty, and when the crowd dispersed it was discovered that they, too, were gone along with Walter Kliebt, whom King JoJo had grabbed, turned upside down, and stuffed down the front of his billowy circus harem pants.

Later, in Milt's car, when it was safe to remove the old actor from his pants, Marty waited for Kliebt's blood pressure to return to normal, which for a ninety-eight-year-old little person is 9/1400, matching, approximately, that of a hummingbird, they then began the uphill battle of putting the best face possible on why one old man in Gypsy clothes and another, even older man in a douche bag hat would abduct a thirty-nine-inch person. Fortunately for the king and Willie Princebone, Walter Kliebt, because he'd been blessed with a loving father, was quick to sympathize with a paternal desperation strong enough to drive a man like Marty to an act of such extremis on behalf of a demented and comatose son. What the dapper little gent found harder to forgive than the kidnapping was the half hour he was forced to spend upside down in such close proximity to Marty's crotch. Marty, a man who'd never had what one might call exemplary bladder control, had, even in the excitement of the kidnapping, forced himself to withhold his natural impulse to spray his victim with urine, a fact for which Mr. Kliebt was, when Marty told him about it, grateful. Gratitude toward a Gypsy, even the king of the Gypsies, for "not flooding me in a river of piss" was one thing, but agreeing to let himself be waved over a nutjob was "a horse of a different color entirely!"

Remarkably, whatever misgivings Kliebt had about the abduction were soon replaced by an exciting, newfound career optimism, which started to bubble within the little old man when Marty revealed that Wagonman and Sloyxne had not always been "of the Gypsy cloth."

"There was a time, not all that long ago," said Milt, "when King JoJo and I were wildly successful Hollywood comedy writer-producers, much beloved by all in the industry!" And, he assured Kliebt, "this ordeal will soon be the guts of a new blockbuster movie" he and King JoJo were preparing, which would star Walter Kliebt as the "centerpoint of the future award-garnering film project!"

Marty even predicted that the finished film would win the Palme d'Or at the Cannes film festival. They spoke of a dynamite young team of hot new writers named Leopold and Sand, who would do the actual writing on this one, and that they—and he, Walter—would executive produce the film, which would "nicely augment, from an economic standpoint," his other duties as love interest to Ann-Margret in the picture.

"All right, you can wave me over your kid. But first . . ."

The midget pointed a half-inch finger up at Marty.

"First, what? You little bast—?" Marty caught himself.

"First . . ." Kliebt's voice sounded like it was emanating from a distant ventriloquist's trunk. "I insist on meeting these two great writers of yours, this Leopold and Loeb. I demanded to meet the writers before signing to appear in *The Wizard of Oz*, and I demand it now before you wave me over anybody. People of all ages are always lifting me and I've had it."

At first, Marty was going to tell the little shit to paint red numbers on his member and take his own anal temperature, but Milt pulled a Wagonman and smoothed the waters.

"Martin, let's go by and see if the boys will help us out here. Tom and Bob have always shown us such devotion . . ." Marty gave Milt a "those guys hate our asses" look, but Milt wisely winked, then nodded quickly toward the old Munchkin.

"Oh, right, Milton, as usual!" King JoJo said, playing along. "Let's swing by and pick up the boys."

Milt and Marty talked themselves through the gates of the studio where Tom and Bob's *Wright for Each Other* was filmed by pretending to be "technical advisers on a Gypsy bounty-hunter movie." The two freshmen Gypsies soon found the correct sound stage and walked right in. When the old men's eyes adjusted to the light, they spotted Leopold and Sand mindlessly grazing the craft services table.

Although Tom and Bob hadn't lived in a tree or become Gypsies, they had gone through a few changes of their own. Due to their lavish lifestyles—i.e., private schools, what with Tom having to pay for his actual children, and Bob donating generous grants to schools that his imaginary kids probably would have been attending, at this point, had he actually sired any—and huge mortgages on their vacation homes alone, Leopold and Sand were forced, after their film careers went down in flames, to return to the day-to-day grind of television work.

Just figureheads at this point, having handed over day-to-day control to the two Buddys after being promised by their newest wunderkind agent, a nineteen-year-old named Yuri Hiamstock, that they'd be the two eight-hundred-pound gorillas of film, Tom and Bob spent their days smoking Cuban cigars and worrying about lip cancer. Oh, they could have wrestled control of the show back but what would have been the point? The Buddys had flushed any artistic quality their creation might once have had down the shitter by filming a three-part episode in which the *Wright for Each Other* plane travels back in time to King Arthur's court and Merlin gets drunk on those tiny bottles of booze.

Tom and Bob were just deciding which bagels looked like they hadn't been groped by every member of a production crew famous for never washing their hands after visiting the bathroom to find Marty aiming a .44 Magnum at them.

"Just listen and don't say anything, boychiks!" said Marty, who demanded in a whisper, as his trademark spittle flew from his mouth onto the bagel Bob had just taken a bite into, that the boys follow him "out to Milt's car, where, we're proud to say, a living *Wizard of Oz* Munchkin is awaiting your arrival. And we've also got enough Hershey bars and Gatorade to get us to Raymond's nuthouse. You remember Raymond, right? My son? You were present, I believe, when I ran out of the writers' room to talk to him when we were all on *Give Your Uncle Back His Legs*, back on your first day in show business, remember?"

"Sure, Marty," said Tom, frozen in place, his eyes locked on Marty's quivering right index finger as it remained wrapped around the .44's trigger.

"How could we ever forget?" asked Bob.

Willie Princebone spoke up. "What King JoJo here is offering you talented boys is a one in a million chance to help pull his Ray-Ray back from a *Wizard of Oz*–induced coma by convincing the actor

Munchkin that you will write a comeback picture for him, which we have already promised him that you'd do. It's the only way he'll agree to wake Raymond up, which I know will happen because the *Wizard of Oz* has always been the father Marty could never be to the boy. No offense meant, Marty."

"None taken," Marty answered. "The story inherent in the script," said Marty, "does not yet exist, but you will manufacture it on the spot—snatch it from inside those beautiful, brilliant heads of yours, if you will, once we get to Milt's car—and it's gotta have heart, not just every minute with the cheap funny ha-ha bullshit, see, but the shit's gotta come from your tickers, it has to move the midget to tears, 'cause if it don't he won't agree to be in it, and if he ain't in it we probably won't be able to sell it, and— Wait, it just occurred to me that while I've been bullshitting with you, the geriatric Munchkin has been sitting inside a hundred-degree car with no fuckin' air comin' his fuckin' way 'cause the fuckin' windows are broken . . ."

"Is King JoJo really asking too much," asked Milt of the boys, looking around at the grandeur of the sound stage with asbestos oozing out of holes in its soundproof walls, "of two guys who, in essence, we started out in a business that's obviously been pretty darned good to them?"

"Not at all," said an increasingly nervous Tom.

"Absolutely not," said an equally terrified Bob.

"Glad to do it," said Tom.

"Absolutely," said Bob. "One question, though. Who's King JoJo?"

What happened next might well be the most unbelievable moment in this otherwise pretty straight ahead and realistic tale. Marty Sloyxne, shaken out of himself by his own parental fear, along with the fear he now realized he himself was stabbing into the hearts of Tom and Bob, two people he really did care about, did something he had never, ever done before—he opened his heart. Yes, Marty Sloyxne, a veritable Mount Everest of horseshit, dropped all his defenses, along with the gun he was holding, but not before showing the guys that it was only a gag gun anyway. Marty then pulled the trigger, unfurling a white flag that read: "B. S. Pully Live Tonight at Skinny D'Amato's 500 Club in Atlantic City."

"Do it again," said Milt, upon seeing the gun for the first time himself.

"Tom, Bob . . ." Marty's words were slow and real and desperate. "My son is sick, guys. He may be dying. The courts ordered him into the medical shit box he lives in and I've never been able to get him sprung. Now they've almost killed him in there. I got to rescue my boy, but I don't have the smarts. I know what I am . . . I'm just a big mouth, a braggart with no class. I know that! But you two guys, you can talk! You're successes, for crying out loud, and people listen to successes. Help me, will ya, fellas? I'm begging you." Marty wiped away a tear. "I know there were times when I made your lives a human shit tower but I also wrestled one of your fathers in a Will You Be My Dad? match, didn't I? I can't remember at this moment which one of your fathers it was but you get my point, and, to the other one of you whose father I didn't wrestle, I say to you: didn't Milt and I inspire you when you were young and had an eating disorder to fill your gut with as much sustenance as you could find? Well, if that doesn't make you want to help us with one small dwarf kidnapping, then you're not the men I think you are!"

Milt, too moved by Marty's eloquence to speak, gently patted Marty on the back. Tom and Bob, their heartbeats returning to the planet earth, looked at each other for a moment and then Bob spoke up. "Tom and I will come, King JoJo, but only if we can keep the B. S. Pully gun."

When Leopold and Sand first entered Milt's car and saw Walter Kliebt, they were stunned to see that the famous Munchkin had turned the same shade of red as the Falcon itself. In the twenty minutes Kliebt had spent locked in the prisoner of war internment camp hot-box atmosphere of the car, the little man had lost 90 percent of his vital fluids, but his disorientation worked in Leopold and Sand's favor, as no explaining needed to be done when the Falcon was pursued in a high-speed chase along the freeway by Highway Patrol, LAPD, and FBI vehicles alerted to the famous midget's kidnapping by the Yamanaguchi news team. Tom and Bob plied the Munchkin with bottled water (each man, in abiding by the unwritten law of the sitcom writer, carried on his person at all times a never-more-than-one-quarter-empty 32-ounce bottle of "purified," overpriced spring water), and Kliebt was revived enough, within twenty minutes' time, to bombard Leopold with questions about the film they were going to write for him. "Now, listen boys," Kliebt proclaimed, "I don't want to play a Munchkin in this one . . . been there, done that, okay?"

By some miracle, Marty's chillingly maniacal driving allowed their pursued vehicle to shake off the coppers before arriving at Raymond's facility. Instead of being frightened by the near death experience of a drive, Kliebt broke into a big grin and said, "This sure beats sitting down in Tallahassee watching my old 'Dean Martin Roast' tapes, fellas."

With the feds and cops temporarily off their asses, the Wagonman Falcon made it inside the gates of Raymond's low-rent mental facility only to find out from the female head administrator of the place that Marty's son had fallen into an even deeper coma, had very little chance of survival, and was allowed only one visitor, "Immediate family only." Stern but professional, the nurse made no mention of Milt's douche bag hat. Marty argued with the nurse, saying that this was the time to "bend the rules a little and let a midget accompany me in there!" But the woman could not be moved.

Milt & Marty

"Y'wanna know your problem, lady?" asked Marty, his cloudy chocolate-brown, degenerate eyes smoldering into her baby blues. "You don't believe in miracles. And when my little Ray-Ray gets midgeted outa that coma of his, it wont even be the first miracle of the day, because the first miracle of the day is that nine hours ago my idiot partner here"—he put his arm gently around Milt's shoulders—"wasn't even a Gypsy!"

Tom and Bob, touched by the logic of Marty's argument, and by the depth of love he so clearly felt for his son, took up his cause.

"Nurse, my name is Tom Leopold. My partner Bob Sand and I created the hit TV series *Wright for Each Other*. If you allow Mr. Sloyxne's smallish friend here to be waved over Raymond, I personally guarantee that we will bus every inmate in this facility, plus the staff and grounds people, down to the studio for a VIP taping of our program."

The polite nurse shook her head. "That's a generous offer, Mr. Leopold, but I really haven't cared for your show since they flew that plane back in time."

Bob ended up saving the day. "How about an autographed director's chair you can bring back here to the mental institution and keep as your very own?"

"Deal," the nurse said, holding up her master key, which Marty snatched with one hand while tucking Walter Kliebt under his arm with the other and flying off, like an arthritic rocket, toward the isolation ward.

With the police and S.W.A.T. sirens on the hospital grounds, there were only seconds left to save Ray-Ray. Milt, Tom, and Bob followed fast in Sloyxne's wake. Leopold and Sand had only seen a photograph of Raymond Errol Flynn Sloyxne and were ill prepared for the sight of the unconscious man lying there, hooked up to a battery of machines. The fifty-two-year-old, hard-muscled baby/man was no more than five feet in height but he'd been blessed with a skull that would have seemed disproportionately large on the body of a seven-footer. When Tom saw Ray, he couldn't believe his eyes; when Bob saw him, he felt less alone in the world.

Once safely gathered around bed 4-C, Marty lifted the Munchkin with one hand and said, "Now it's time for me to work some Gypsy magic before the feds break in here and do something tragic." Using Kliebt's tiny quivering form the way a magician might use a wand, he passed the little man back and forth three times over Ray-Ray's unconscious form, while chanting the Vivica or the Gypsy Life Reinstatement Prayer. "As Gypsy king I have the might to reverse all wrongs and make 'em right and I will never end the fight to bring my Ray-Ray to the light."

To which Milt replied, "And now he'll come alive methinks, so we can all go out and eat some Chinks."

Nothing. No response. If anything, the chant seemed only to make Raymond more unconscious. Marty sang it again and louder but again to no avail. The sound of angry footsteps of the law on linoleum inching toward them made Marty more desperate than he'd ever been in his life. "Wake up, you lazy pile of shit!" he screamed at his son. "Get your thirty-pound head outa that bed right now or I swear to God I'm going to kick your chubby heinie over the Grauman's Chinese Theatre!" There was a moment of silence and then, miraculously, Raymond's eyes slowly opened.

The men around the bed gasped. Tears poured down Marty's cheeks as Raymond spoke for the first time in days to the man who had, once more, given him life. "Who the fuck do you think you're yelling at, Dad, you fucking old failure?" Ray-Ray said, so happy to see his father that, for a moment, he became him.

"My son, my son!" Marty fell to his knees and sobbed gratefully to the heavens. "My kinderloch has come back to me!"

The authorities kicked down the door at that very moment and started intimidating everybody. Not Walter Kliebt, however, who, it was discovered, had been the smallest and oldest man ever to graduate from the U.S. Navy SEAL training academy. Milt and Marty, however, were pounced on by members of the California Highway Patrol and the FBI, shoulder-rolled, and thrown into handcuffs. The good news? Walter Kliebt refused to press kidnapping charges against Wagonman and Sloyxne after Tom and Bob promised to sign him to play a recurring character in their pilot called *Gilbert*, as a ninety-year-old, unusually wise, half-blind air safety controller. "I hope you understand," said Bob, "that *Gilbert* is just a pilot right now and the only way you'll get to play your role is if the network picks it up as a series."

"Relax, kid," said Kliebt. "It's a great idea and it's gonna go. In the meantime, let's talk about that movie you and the skinny kid wanna write for me."

And so, with nothing to charge anybody with (after all, it's not a crime in America to wear a douche bag on your head), the police had no choice but to release JoJo and Princebone back into an unsuspecting, Gypsy-fearing population.

There was a moment, though, there in that place, on that day, when Leopold and Sand fully realized that they had, after all these years, finally been set free of the Wagonman and Sloyxne curse. Risking life and reputation for Marty, and therefore for Milt, they had removed forever the two sociopathic thorns from their collective paw. But—and here may be the oddest wrap-up a story ever had—Tom and Bob no longer wanted to be set free. As they moved off into the hospital background and watched while insane people and medical staff celebrated Marty and Ray-Ray's reunion with a facility-wide party featuring blue Jell-O, sugarless whipped cream, soundless whistles, party hats that the patients wore everywhere but on their heads, and a ventriloquist act featuring an elderly patient named Roy whose "dummy" was an elderly catatonic woman nicknamed Precious, Tom and Bob were struck and totally surprised by the deep sense of love they had come to feel for the two old men. They felt for them as one comes to feel about family. *Milt and Marty may be untalented, crazy, old, never-was psychopaths,* they thought, *but they're our untalented, crazy, old psychopaths!* It was at this moment that Tom and Bob decided to honor Wagonman and Sloyxne with a tribute both undeserved and long overdue.

It took Tom and Bob some doing to get the Friars Club to readmit Milt and Marty to its ranks. For starters, the club made Milt and Marty renounce any allegiance to the Gypsies and, for seconds, Tom and Bob had to donate the cost ($70,000) of a room dedicated to the boys. It was to be named the Wagonman and Sloyxne Pantry and was to be located just off the kitchen. It would be a sanctuary of sorts where Marty Sloyxne would be allowed to lick the sourdough powder off loaves of bread for the remainder of his days, and should Milt outlive his partner then Marty's licking rights would revert to Milt.

As if they hadn't done enough, Tom and Bob pulled a few Hollywood strings and got Ray-Ray moved to a more modern hospital facility just blocks from the Friars Club. This new institution provided Raymond with cutting-edge medication designed to wean him from the addictive *Wizard of Oz* teat.

Still, even a Friars Roast in their honor didn't feel sufficient enough an homage for two men who had revolutionized failure and had come to mean so much to Tom and Bob, two guys with a dream that Milt and Marty had lit a fire under before abusing them and frightening their families half to death.

Once upon a time, Tom and Bob were just childhood fans, and now they were fast approaching the same age Milt and Marty had been when they first started stalking Tom and Bob. And so, they felt, it was only right that Milt and Marty should not only have a place to go every day (the Friars), but also have their place in the sun.

At first they couldn't give tickets away for the "Friars Club Roasts Milt and Marty: The Longest Lasting and Least Successful Comedy Writing Duo in Show Biz History." Most of the people the team started out with were either dead, hated them too much to attend, or so old they forgot how much they despised them but were too crippled to make it to the club anyway. So the bulk of the gala's audience (forty people) was made up of Friars staff; people from the garment industry and real estate who now made up most of the once all–show business club's roster; Tom and his wife, Bob and "his Barbara," a raw vegetable artist he'd met and for whom he was falling fast; Gwen and their recently reconciled lesbian daughter, Randi, along with Randi's "husband" Frank, who had just recovered from full reconstructive surgery and possessed if not a working penis, then something very close to one—and a surprise guest.

Although Marty was touched by all the love he felt in the room, it didn't stop him from berating the crowd for "not even being in the fucking Business!" Just then the doors swung open and a much more mentally healthy Raymond came in, approached the dais, and roasted his dad with a joke written by Tom and Bob. "I have the meanest dog in the world," he said. "He ain't got no asshole." Then, in a different voice, Ray-Ray continued: "If he ain't got no asshole, how does he shit? He can't," Ray-Ray said in his regular voice. "That's what makes him so mean!" Marty dissolved in tears, expressing for the first time in his life his love for Raymond . . . not to mention the same theretofore unexpressed emotion for Milt, Gwen, and Tom and Bob, while then quickly shifting gears and berating Ray-Ray for his "lousy timing and delivery of some very solid middle of the road material!"

And so the circle was complete. Four men, born half a century apart, two with talent and good fortune, two with nothing more than bad prostates and a "joy in the work," who'd transcended the "surly bonds of earth" to come together, this night, on a heavily mortgaged plot of land called the Friars Club West not just to honor two not quite grand old men but, in a way, to do honor to their own sense of forgiveness . . . and to the business that gave all of their lives meaning—not to mention the opportunity to shvitz naked in the finest, mentholated steam room in town.

Less than two weeks later, however, Milt and Marty were once again banned for life from the Friars when Marty was caught stealing six sets of blue velvet drapes off the Sinatra Room windows. "I was just going to make some new lucky pants for my partner. Is that so wrong?" Marty protested to the board. "The man's keester looks rounder in blue velvet and round is in, my friends!"

ACKNOWLEDGMENTS

|||||||||||||||||||||||||||||

I'd like to thank Judy Twersky for leading us to Ken Siman. Ken, you made it a better book and we thank you! And I'd like to thank Drew Friedman for the great cover art. We spent the whole book trying to live up to it! Thanks also to Marc Dworkin. And Bob? It's been a gas.

—*Tom Leopold*

I want to thank the following people for their love, support, encouragement, and, of course, senses of humor: Darren Sand, Wendy Sand, Eric Vizents, Monica Erickson, Kaye Jacobs-Giorgio, Tony Giorgio, Jay Sand, Maryse Sand, Alexandra Vizents, Audrey Sand, Katherine Sand, and, of course, Tom Leopold, without whom this book would be only half of what it is . . . And I want to thank the following person for having had the courage to publish and edit this book: Ken Siman.

—*Bob Sand*